Handmade Style: Shaker

Handmade Style

Shaker

by Dorothy Wood

Photographs by Lucinda Symons

CHRONICLE BOOKS

SAN FRANCISCO

First published in the United States in 1999 by Chronicle Books.

Text copyright © 1999 by Dorothy Wood.
Photographs © 1999 by Lucinda Symons.

Library of Congress Cataloging-in-Publication Data:

Wood, Dorothy.
    Shaker : simple projects and inspiration for the home / by Dorothy Wood ;
        photographs by Lucinda Symons.
    p. cm. – (Handmade style)
    ISBN 0-8118-2568-X
    1. Handicraft—United States. 2. Shaker art—United States. I. Title. II. Series.
TT23.W66 1999
745.5—dc21   99-14413
                          CIP

Printed in Italy

Distributed in Canada by Raincoast Books
8680 Cambie Street
Vancouver, British Columbia V6P 6M9

10 9 8 7 6 5 4 3 2 1

Chronicle Books
85 Second Street
San Francisco, California 94105

www.chroniclebooks.com

contents

introduction

Is it not incredible that a group of people, who lived and worked together in the mid-19th century, should have had such a profound influence on modern design? Although considered outré in its time, the furnishings and accessories of the Shaker movement inspired the Bauhaus School of Architecture, itself the "father of modernism," to such an extent that their slogan "Form follows function" is a direct take-off from the Shaker dictum "Beauty rests on Utility." Just as the Shakers believed that "All beauty that has not a foundation in use soon grows distasteful and needs continual replacement with something new," in the 1920s the Bauhaus School taught that if something is designed to fit its purpose, beauty will look after itself. Yet I am sure we can all think of examples of perfectly functional objects that are in actual fact quite ugly, so how and why did the Shakers make such beautiful things? The Shakers themselves had one simple answer to this apparent conundrum. They regarded the creative spirit as a gift, and believed that "if you improve in one talent, God will give you more."

The Shakers, more formally known as the United Society of Believers, were the largest and most successful of a number of religious sects that were active in the United States of America at the beginning of the 19th century. The group was founded by a young British woman, Ann Lee, who emigrated to America in 1774. Many of the "laws" of the Shaker community were directly related to the poor quality of life that she had left behind in Britain, and her desire to begin anew. Ann Lee wanted to create a Utopia where people could live together in equality, fraternity, and peace. It was not easy for new converts to adjust to the celibate, communal life, but they were introduced to it in stages, much

as a novice nun or monk is introduced to the convent or monastery. The Shakers lived together in "families" of between ten and one hundred members. Each family was a separate entity, with its own dwelling house, work shops, and barns. The Brothers and Sisters lived together in the dwelling house, but they had separate retiring rooms, and they entered by different doors. Each community comprised between two and eight families, living about a quarter of a mile (400m) apart. The families were named after the location of their dwelling house in relation to the meeting house, such as the "North" family, or after their main occupation, such as the "Mill" family.

INTRODUCTION

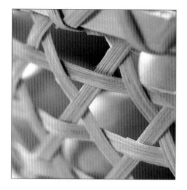

The Shaker communities were highly structured. Unlike the "outside world," they were egalitarian but not democratic. There were Elders and Eldresses to oversee spiritual and personal concerns, and experienced Deacons and Deaconesses to supervise work in the fields, kitchens, and workshops. These senior members of the society were chosen on the basis of virtue and competence, and were expected to lead by example. This simple system of government, which relied on the goodness of mankind, was remarkably successful although not without problems. In order to maintain and preserve the vow of celibacy, the Shakers led very regulated lives. The Sisters and Brothers worked on different tasks, returning to the dwelling house for lunch and the evening meal. Even then they were segregated, sitting on opposite sides of the dining rooms. There were social gatherings, but these were organized in strict rotation so that the Brothers and Sisters did not get the opportunity to become close.

Mother Ann Lee asked only that they put their "hands to work and [their] hearts to God." Freed from the constraints of normal life, the Shakers had an opportunity for creativity that most of us can only dream of. With finances buoyed by trade with the "outside world" in crops, herbs and furniture, they had ample workspace, the best materials, and an inspiring environment in which to work. They were under no pressure to make a profit and could give each piece the time and effort required to make it perfect. The Shakers had to learn to be patient – after all they were creating for the Millenium: "Do all your work as though you had a thousand years to live, and as you would if you knew you must die tomorrow." The essence of any Shaker object, whether a piece of furniture or an accessory, can be captured by just three words – simplicity, utility, and precision. Each item was plain, functional, and well made, but also had a subtle beauty that relied almost entirely on its shape and proportions.

The community at New Lebanon, New York, was the model for all other communities and shaped the visual world of the Shakers, in terms of their clothing, artifacts, and buildings. Mother Ann Lee believed that the outward appearance of things revealed the inner spirit, and her teachings were the basis of the Millenial Laws that covered all aspects of community life. There were rules for worship, work – even eating – and also detailed restrictions on the making of goods. "Movables," for example, could be painted in particular colors, while other wood furniture could only be varnished; mirrors could be no larger than 12 x 18in (30 x 45cm); and bedcovers were to be woven from no more than two colors.

The unique style of the Shaker furnishings and accessories did not emerge overnight, but evolved gradually, and not without a great deal of trial and error. Initially there was little to distinguish the style of the rest of society from that of the Shaker communities, but as the fashions "outside" began to embrace more ornate, decorative ideas, the Shakers continued to refine their plain and simple designs. The Brothers and Sisters were free to experiment with different materials and proportions, so that, by the time of the "Golden Age" (1820–1850) – the peak of the movement's popularity – the Shaker style in furniture and artifacts, regarded today as a hallmark of good design, had become established.

The Shaker communities were seen as an everlasting institution, looking after the physical and spiritual needs of believers for the whole of their natural lives. Numbers began to dwindle after 1860, however, and have continued to drop until now there are only a handful of believers in the community at Sabbathday Lake, Maine. Mother Ann Lee's prediction that "There will come a time when there won't be enough believers to bury their own dead" has almost come about. She believed that there would be a revival when only five believers were left. Perhaps this revival is taking another form, as Sister Frances Carr from Sabbath-day Lake explains: "We'll go away in time, as will everybody, but our ideas and our way of life will never go away." Today, more and more people are becoming familiar with Shaker products. Craftsmen and women are continuing to make fur-niture and artifacts in the Shaker tradition and the public are increas-ingly willing to pay that little bit extra for a true work of art.

The aim of this book is not to recreate Shaker design per se, but to capture its essence and so create items for our homes that are simple, elegant, and timeless. In a world of mass-production and dwindling quality, a return to that which is handmade and precision-crafted has enormous appeal. I have included designs for furniture, containers, linens, and a delightful range of accessories. If there is one thing common to all the projects, it is that I have chosen plain, quality materials to create useful objects of classic simplicity. The diversity of the projects – which involve metalwork, wirework, wood-work, sewing, and knitting – ensures that there is something for everyone, and every home. When you choose to make one of the projects in the book, don't try and finish it as quickly as possible; instead, allow yourself enough time to make it really well.

If you are interested in finding out more about the Shaker way of life, in the United States of America you can visit Shaker villages at Hancock, New England and Canterbury, New Hampshire, and Shaker museums in Old Chatham, New York and South Union, Kentucky. In the United Kingdom, The American Museum at Calverton, Bath has a Shaker Room and an extensive library on the subject.

putting it together

Creating a Shaker look doesn't require great artistic skills because the style relies on simple designs with a minimum of decoration. Today, electric tools take much of the hard work out of woodworking and sewing, allowing you to make things easily and accurately. Providing you have the right tools for the job, you should be able to try any of the projects in this book.

I have designed the wood projects around basic shapes and simple joints so that most can be cut with a tenon saw. Curved edges can also be cut with a fret saw but, because it takes practice to saw wood accurately by hand, access to a band saw or jigsaw will make the task easier. A circular saw is needed to cut the larger pieces for the dining bench and tray table. Alternatively, for a small fee, your local lumber yard will cut and trim pieces of wood to a particular size, ready for use.

It is worth investing in a basic tool kit so that you have the tools to complete most of the woodworking projects. This should contain: a measuring tape; T square; set of wood drill bits size $1/16$-$3/8$in/ 1-10mm; electric or rechargeable drill; countersink; range of wood screws; wood glue; sanding block; different grades of sanding paper; tenon saw; hand saw; screwdrivers to suit the screws; small nails; hammer; nail punch; "G" clamp; masking tape; wood filler; and dust mask.

The Shaker box and tray table are perhaps the most challenging projects to make because you must use special tools. A router is needed to cut the joints for the sloping table surround, and a circular saw, set at an angle, to cut the top. The quintessential Shaker box requires a band saw, and a disc sander to allow you to shape accurately the forming block, the box base, and the lid.

For the fabric projects you will need the basic sewing kit (needles; pins; sewing thread; scissors; seam unpicker; and measuring tape), and a sewing machine for long seams. I think the most important tool for these projects is an iron. It is essential to press each stage as you go, to ensure that seams lie flat and hems and turnings are straight before you stitch.

When working with wire and metal buy the best quality tools you can afford. Sharp, heavyweight tin snips will cut tin plate with a straight, clean edge and, with a good set of wire cutters and pliers, you can easily cut and bend the heavy galvanized wire.

Finally, a word about safety. Don't forget to wear safety goggles when doing wirework, protective gloves when cutting metal, and a dust mask when working with Medium Density Fiberboard (MDF).

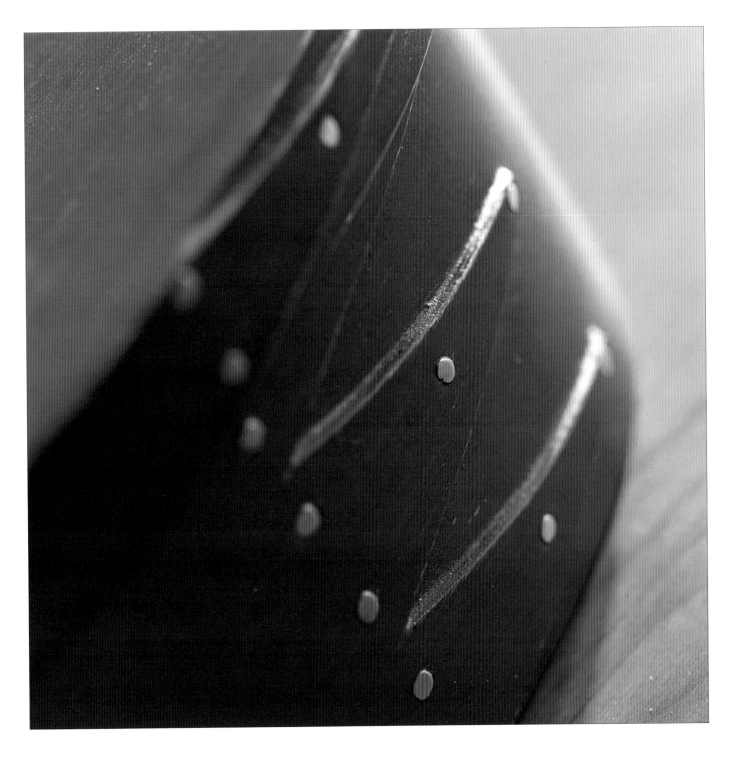

PUTTING IT TOGETHER

linens

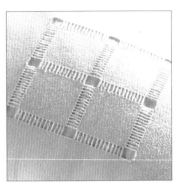

A s with all things Shaker, the linens used in the community were made to exacting standards of simplicity and excellence. Fabrics such as plain raw or bleached linen, crisp white cotton and classic checks and stripes have a timeless appeal and can be used to make a variety of stylish and elegant linens, bed covers, and soft furnishings. Each of the projects in this chapter has been made with the same attention to detail and form that distinguishes a Shaker-made object from cheaper, second-rate goods.

The table runner is made from top quality linen, finished with a deep double hem and mitered corners, and features a delicate bird motif as a subtle decorative touch. The elegant proportions of the table runner will complement the simple lines of any plain wood table. This harmony between shape and form can transform even the humble pillow case into an object of grace and beauty. Drawn-thread embroidery is used to create a simple geometric pattern on a pure white cotton pillow case, made in the classic Oxford style with deep hems and crisp mitered corners.

Like the Shakers, many of us are keen to create an uncluttered but comfortable environment in which to live. Although the style, then as now, avoids fussy detail, favoring instead clean lines and elegant proportions, it is not cold and unwelcoming: plain fabrics and furniture can be offset by check and striped fabrics; a couple of matching cushions can be used to add a touch of color and comfort to

a plain Shaker chair; and a basket-weave hand towel and toilet bag can introduce pleasing textures to a modern bathroom.

Since the colors used for Shaker fabrics were mixed from basic vegetable dyes, they tended to be muted, and therefore different colors worked well together. The soft sage green and red I used for the cushion covers are typical Shaker colors that complement each other beautifully, in defiance of the old adage "red and green should never be seen." The soft and warm quilt, made in classic Shaker blue and white, has a quiet beauty which relies on the choice of materials and the way in which they are put together.

LINENS

quilt

Since Millenial Laws stipulated that only two colors could be used for bed covers, the Shakers wove blankets in check patterns, most often in blue, red or black on a white ground. While they were not renowned for their quilts, the simplicity of the square block construction is very much in keeping with the Shaker ethic, and the homespun pure cotton fabrics I have chosen are very similar to the check fabrics they wove themselves.

The finished quilt has an antique, puckered look because the cotton batting stitched inside the quilt is designed to shrink when the quilt is first washed. The quilt layers are stitched by machine along the patch-work seams. The batting bounces back on either side after stitching to create a ditch, and so this technique is known as "in the ditch" quilting. It is worked with quilter's invisible thread, which makes it look hand quilted.

The quilting of the large cream squares is completed by hand. The simple Shaker house motif that decorates these large squares is taken from one of the many maps that show the layout of the Shaker communities. These early maps were naively drawn without perspective – some of the houses drawn upside down or even balanced on the roofs of others – but they still provide a precious lasting record of the Shaker way of life.

As a finishing touch, the quilt is bound with strips cut from a large check fabric in the same two colors as the patchwork fabric.

The nine-patch quilt is made from three different blocks, arranged to form a subtle diamond pattern. If you can't find the correct width of muslin at your fabric store, sew two narrower pieces together to make the backing.

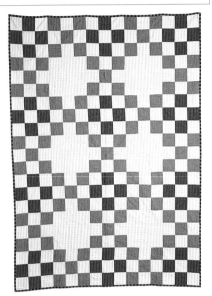

MATERIALS
◆ ¾yd/0.75m and 1yd/1m of two small check homespun fabrics
◆ ½yd/0.5m of a larger check home-spun fabric
◆ 2¾yd/2.5m of 108in/2.75m wide natural American muslin
◆ 60 x 85in/152 x 215cm cotton batting
◆ Rotary cutter, mat and quilting ruler
◆ Cream cotton thread
◆ Quilter's invisible thread
◆ Strong quilting thread
◆ Sewing machine and sewing kit
◆ Iron
◆ Paper and pencil

Finished size: about 57 x 79½in/145 x 202cm

1 Press the patchwork fabric with a steam iron to remove any creases. Fold and press the selvages together, matching the checks in both layers. Turn the folded edge up to the selvage edge and press. Make sure that the checks run parallel in each layer.

2 Allow the fabric to cool and then lift onto the cutting mat. Align the pressed fold with one marked line on the ruler. Hold the ruler firmly in place and cut off the uneven edge of the fabric.

3 Work across the fabric, cutting 4½in/11.5cm wide strips. Open out the first strip to check that you are cutting straight and that the checks are aligned through the layers.

4 Turn the first strip until it is horizontal. Straighten the end in the same way as before. Cut 4½in/11.5cm squares from the strip. Cut 48 squares in one small check and 85 squares in the other.
(see picture next column)

5 Cut 128 4½in/11.5cm muslin squares. Use the 48 check squares and the muslin squares to speed piece the first set of blocks. Sew a check and muslin square together with right sides facing. Use the side of the presser foot as a guide to make a ¼in/6mm seam.

6 Without breaking the thread, feed the next two patches under the presser foot, the other way up, and then stitch the last pair in the same way as the first. This block has four check and five cream squares.

7 Add a cream square to the other side of the first pair, a check square to the middle row, and a cream square to the last row. You now have a block held together with thread ties. Make another 11 blocks the same.

8 Snip the first block apart and press the seams in each row towards the dark fabric. Pin the rows together with right sides facing, matching the seam lines.

9 Sew the rows together and press the seams into the center. Using the other small check fabric, make 17 blocks with five check squares and four cream squares. Press as before.

10 The blocks will be approximately 12¼in/31cm square. Cut 6 cream squares the same size. Begin to piece the blocks together. Pin a four check block to a five check block, matching the seams, and sew together.

11 The first row has a four, five, four, five, four block pattern. Make three more rows like this. The second row has a five, cream, five, cream, five block pattern. Make two more rows like this.

12 When the seven rows are complete, press the seams again. Then, starting with a four, five, four, five, four row and alternating the two patterns, join the rows to make the quilt.

13 Press the completed quilt top thoroughly from both sides. Measure the quilt top. Cut batting and a muslin backing to size. Lay the batting over the backing, then smooth the patchwork quilt on top. Start in the center and tack lines out to the edges through all layers.

14 Tack again around every second row of squares to hold the layers together securely. Fill the bobbin with cream cotton and thread the machine with invisible thread. Loosen the top tension slightly and stitch "in the ditch" between the squares. (*see picture next column*)

15 Roll the quilt under the head of the machine as you go. Do not stitch the large squares. Complete all the stitching in one direction and then turn the quilt to stitch the other sides of the squares.

16 Enlarge the house template at the back of the book. Transfer in pencil onto the large cream squares. Hand quilt along the lines using a strong quilting thread. Trim the batting and backing to the same size as the quilt top.

17 Cut 2⅜in/6cm wide strips, two the exact width of the quilt and two 1½in/4cm longer than the length. With right sides facing and ¼in/6mm seams, sew the binding to the short edges. Fold the binding over the raw edge, turn under a seam allowance and hem stitch on the wrong side. Repeat for the long sides, folding in the extra tabs at each end and oversewing the corners neatly. Wash in warm water to remove any pencil lines.

t a b l e
r u n n e r

The Shakers used no surface decoration on furniture and household goods but found an outlet for artistic expression in their inspirational drawings. These beautiful and detailed watercolors were created by those Brothers and Sisters who believed they had received spiritual messages from their dead founder, Mother Ann Lee. The drawings were not meant for display, but were sent as greetings and messages to other members of the community. They often featured an assortment of motifs, described in tiny poems and pieces of prose, and were laid out with characteristic order and precision. The bird on a branch was a recurring theme and often had a rhyming inscription such as "I am a Dove of Comfort and Love."

This elegant table runner has been lightly stenciled using pale gray paint, so that the delicate bird on a branch motif shows up against the white linen. If you prefer to uphold the strict ethics of the Shakers, who did not use tablecloths to show that their tables were "clean enough to eat on without cloths," you could use the stencil to decorate a curtain or simple flat blind instead.

The beauty of the stenciled motif lies in its subtlety; it is a decorative touch which does not detract from the clean lines of the table runner.

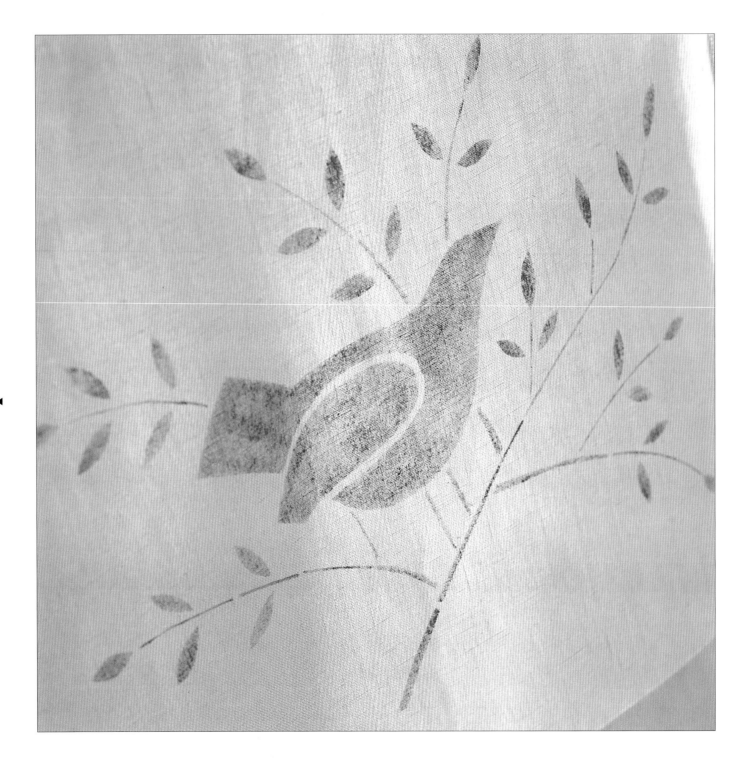

The neat ordered appearance of this table runner relies on the accurate turning and sewing of the hems and mitered corners. Spray the finished project with starch and press for a really crisp finish.

SEWING MACHINE SKILLS REQUIRED

MATERIALS

◆ 2¾yd/2.5m Zweigart Edinburgh linen
◆ Sewing kit and sewing machine
◆ Mylar plastic
◆ Light gray stencil paint
◆ Craft knife and cutting mat
◆ Stencil brush
◆ Spray adhesive
◆ Masking tape
◆ Paper and pencil
◆ Paper towel
◆ Iron

Finished size: 24in/61cm x length required

1 Wash the linen in lukewarm water and liquid detergent to pre-shrink it and to remove any surface finish. Iron while still damp. Cut a strip of linen 31½in/80cm wide to fit across your table, allowing 31½in/80cm to hang down each side. These measurements include seam allowances.

2 Turn under and press a double 2in/5cm hem on all sides. Open out the hem and fold over the corners exactly where the outside creases meet. Cut across this fold line. Press with the iron. Tack the hem and mitered corners in place. (see picture next column)

The simple bird motif is easy to stencil using the template at the back of the book.

3 From the right side, machine stitch along the edge of the hem to secure. Slip stitch the mitered corners neatly.

4 Enlarge the template at the back of the book to the required size. Place it on the cutting mat and tape the Mylar plastic on top. Carefully cut along the lines to cut out the stencil.

5 Tape one end of the table runner to a clean surface. Spray the wrong side of the stencil with spray adhesive and position centrally at the end of the table runner.

6 Take some gray paint on the end of the stencil brush and dab off the excess onto a piece of paper towel. Dab the paint onto the stencil, building up the color slowly so that it doesn't bleed under the stencil.

7 Peel off the stencil and allow the paint to dry. Use a medium hot iron on the reverse side to set the paint. This usually takes about 5 minutes. Stencil the other end of the table runner to match.

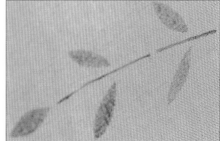

cushion covers

Seating in the Shaker communities was not uphol-stered, although some of the wooden benches used in the meeting rooms had seat cushions, probably for use by the elderly members.

Fabrics were woven by the Brothers and Sisters as well as being bought in from the "Outside World," so it is difficult to ascertain whether fabrics used on such cushions are authentic "Shaker" or not. Howev-er, we know that they used only two color hues in any one fabric and that the gradations formed by the weave allowed them to produce a variety of beautiful fabrics. The threads were dyed using the simple Shak-er palette that included the soft sage green, blood red and pale creamy yellow used to make these cush-ions. Stripes usually appeared as striped borders on individual cloths and neckerchiefs but are in keeping with the Shaker preference for uncomplicated geomet-ric patterns and design.

These flap cushions have simple loop and but-ton or tie fastenings and are carefully designed so that there is no complicated matching of patterns. Com-bine a stripe and check fabric, as here, or try a large and small check for a slightly different effect.

For the tie on this cushion, two lengths of cord are worked through the gaps in the weave, one on the flap and one on the main cushion cover, and the ends are knotted inside out of sight.

```
                   WINNERS!
         EVERYBODY LOVES A WINNER
              #286, ST. ALBERT
               780-418-6363
      GST NO. 86032 6255 RT0001 CA#07043

CUSTOMER SALE            0286/0003/3357-6
8661 cashier             JAN-26-03 15:24

81 STAT./BODY & BATH
281778    1@ 3.00               3.00G

    1 ITEMS SUBTOTAL            3.00
    3.00 TAX GST 7%             0.21

      TOTAL                     3.21
         CASH                  20.21
      DUE CUSTOMER
           CHANGE              17.00

     * REFUNDS WITHIN 10 DAYS *
         * WITH RECEIPT *
    THANK YOU FOR SHOPPING AT WINNERS!
```

The two cushion covers are made in the same way. The instructions below are for the button fastening. For a tie fastening, thread lengths of cord through a gap in the weave and tie knots on the inside to secure. Attach the other pieces on the edge of the flap instead of loops.

▶ 27

SEWING MACHINE SKILLS REQUIRED

MATERIALS
- *20 x 40in/51 x 102cm striped Indian cotton*
- *20 x 25in/51 x 64cm check Indian cotton*
- *18in/45cm square cushion pad*
- *Three ¾in/2cm buttons*
- *½yd/0.5m cord*
- *Sewing kit and sewing machine*
- *Iron*

Finished size: to fit 18in/45cm square cushion

1 Cut a piece of striped fabric 16 x 18in/40 x 45cm with the stripes going lengthways. Cut a piece 18 x 20in/45 x 51cm with the stripes going widthways.

2 Cut a 18 x 25in/45 x 64cm piece of check fabric. The rib of the cloth must face in the same direction in each piece.

3 Fold three 5in/13cm pieces of cord in half and pin, evenly spaced, along the top edge of the check fabric.

4 With right sides together, pin the small striped piece on top of the check fabric, enclosing the loops.
(see picture next column)

Carefully determine the position of each button on the cushion cover before sewing it on with a long shank, allowing for the thickness of the cord loop.

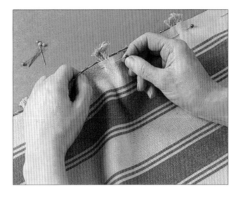

5 Measure and mark 8in/20cm down each side. Machine stitch round the flap between the marks, catching in the loops as you come to them. Reverse stitch at each end.

6 Trim the seams and across the corners. Snip into the seam allowance where the stitching ends and turn the flap through. Ease out the corners and press flat.

7 Turn under 2in/5cm along the top edge of the remaining striped fabric and pin to the check fabric, matching the

turned edge to the top of the seam allowances. Sew around the three sides, reverse stitching at each end for strength. Zigzag the first 1in/2.5 cm and trim neatly.

8 Fold the cushion flap and pin in position. Mark the position of the three buttons. Sew on each button with a shank to accommodate the thickness of the cord loop.

pillow case

Bed linen in the dwelling houses did not belong to any one individual but to the family as a whole. Each piece was clearly marked to identify the family, often with just a single letter, such as "S" for the South family. The linens were stored in large communal cupboards to keep them clean and fresh. The cupboards themselves, designed so that the spacing of the shelves and depth of the drawers suited the contents, were built to exacting standards both inside and out.

Bed linen was plain, simple, and unadorned, but the ordered appearance of drawn-thread work adheres to the Shaker ideal.

This pillow case is made almost entirely by hand, with the hem stitch grouping the drawn threads into bars as well as holding the flange in place. Choose a medium-weight good quality cotton muslin or fine linen so that the threads are quite distinct and easy to pull out. If the fabric is not of an even weave you will find that the square sides have an unequal number of threads.

The simple design on crisp white muslin will complement any bed linen. Make up two and use them as a decorative feature at the head of the bed.

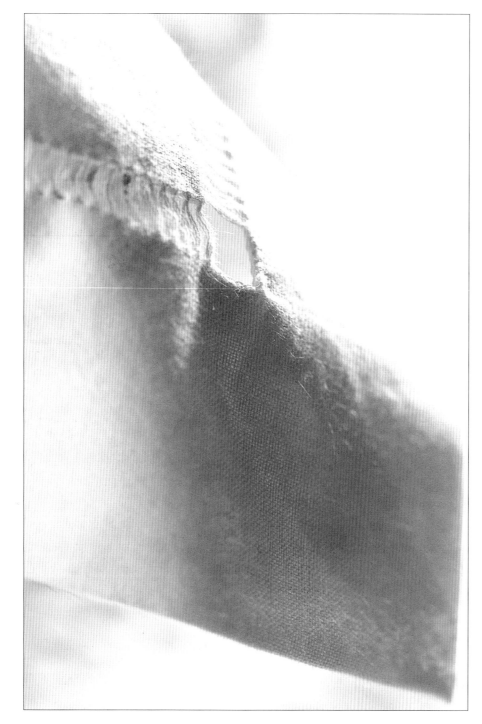

This beautiful drawn-thread work cushion can be stitched entirely by hand in two or three days. A magnifying lamp makes counting and drawing threads and working the hem stitch much easier.

MATERIALS
◆ 2¼yd/2m of 44in/112cm wide cotton muslin
◆ 27in/68.5cm square pillow
◆ Sewing kit and sewing machine
◆ White sewing thread
◆ Pencil and paper
◆ Iron
◆ Starch

Finished size: about 30in/76cm square

1 From the muslin, cut a 35½in/90cm square and two pieces 22 x 28in/ 55 x 70cm.

2 Make a light pencil dot in each corner of the square, 4in/10cm from the sides. This marks the outside line of the drawn-thread work.

3 Measure 1½in/4cm from the dot, cut across a few threads and carefully lift the threads out as far as the dot. Draw out 16 threads in all.
(see picture next column)

Threads are grouped into bundles of six as the hem is stitched. If you have not tried drawn-thread work before, follow the diagram for hem stitch on page 104.

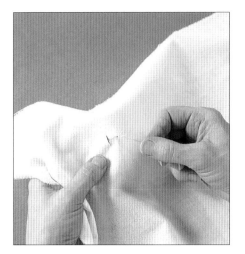

4 Draw the top thread out towards the dot in the next corner. Stop about 1½in/4cm away from the dot and snip the thread. Cut across the threads as before and lift out 16 threads in total.

5 Continue around the square, pulling out the same 16 threads, and leaving 1½in/4cm tails at each corner.

6 Cut six 4in/10cm squares of paper and arrange them in two rows on the fabric square. Mark the corners of the squares. Remove 16 threads round each square in the same way as before.

7 Take out 16 threads across the center of each square to make four smaller squares. Hem stitch along each edge gathering the threads into bundles of 6. Trim the drawn threads and work buttonhole stitch along the raw edges.

8 Turn under and press ¼in/6mm along each side of the muslin square and fold the edges over until they meet the outside line of the drawn threads. Press the fold.

9 Open out the hem and fold over the corner exactly where the pressed lines meet. Trim the corner tab to ¼in/6mm and refold the hem, mitering the corners neatly. Trim the long threads at the corner and tuck into the hem. Tack the hem.

10 Working from the right side, hem stitch along the edge of the drawn threads, gathering them into bundles of 6 threads and catching in the hem as you go. Slip stitch the mitered corners.

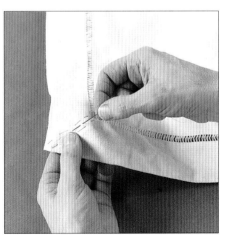

11 Turn under a ½in/1.5cm hem along one long side of each of the other pieces of fabric and machine stitch. Press under ¼in/6mm on the other three sides.

12 Lay the fabric square face down. Lay the rectangles on top, right sides up, so that the hems overlap and the pressed edges fit exactly inside the drawn threads. Pin and tack in place.

13 Sew around the inside edge of the drawn threads with hem stitch, gathering the same 6 threads into bars and catching in the pillow case back as you go. Oversew a few stitches where the envelope opens.

14 Spray the finished pillow case with starch and press.

15 The hand-stitching on this pillow case makes it unsuitable for machine washing. Instead, hand wash and roll in a towel to remove excess moisture and press while still slightly damp.

hand towel
and
toilet bag

Just like their contemporaries elsewhere in America and in Great Britain, young Sisters stitched samplers to improve their sewing and embroidery skills. The Shaker samplers were used to practice letters and numbers for marking the clothes and linens used in the communities. This was essential because the Brothers and Sisters lived in family groups of up to a hundred members. The large dwelling houses had separate sleeping accommodation for Brothers and Sisters and all the linen and spare clothing was stored in large cupboards. Bed linen and towels were marked with the name of the family and clothes bore discreet labels with the wearer's initials.

The Shakers' orderliness and attention to detail was reflected even in their embroidery: they used marking cross stitch to stitch initials. In this reversible method of working cross stitch, a square of stitches forms on the wrong side, making the back as neat as the front. You can use ordinary cross stitch for the toilet bag as it is lined, but it is best to use the more time-consuming method for the hand towel.

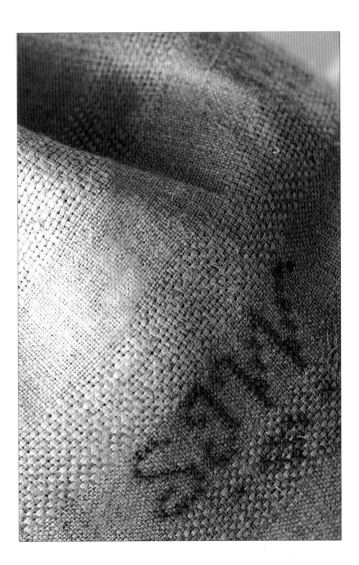

▶ 33

Use a simple cross stitch for the initials and heart motif on the toilet bag. Use the diagram on page 105 as a guide for stitching your own initials, or those of a relative or friend.

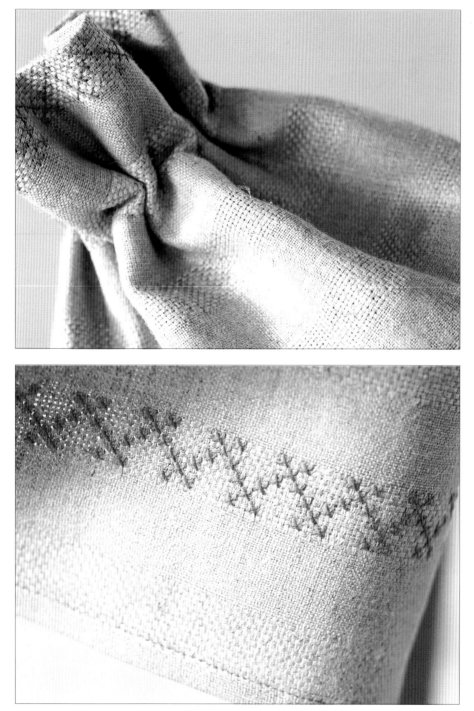

Bray linen has distinctive basket weave stripes running across the fabric, but any even-weave raw linen will be suitable for this project. Use flower thread for the stitching as it has a rustic feel that complements the linen.

BASIC EMBROIDERY SKILLS REQUIRED

MATERIALS

◆ 1yd/1m Bray linen
◆ 12 x 22in/30 x 56cm brushed cotton lining
◆ DMC 2434 flower thread
◆ 1yd/1m cord
◆ Sewing kit and sewing machine

Finished size (towel): about 17½ x 27½in/44.5 x 70cm
(bag): about 10¾in x 12in/27 x 30cm

1 Cut a piece of linen 18 x 28in/46 x 71cm. Press under ¼in/6mm along each edge. Turn under a further ¼in/ 6mm down each long side and machine stitch close to the fold. Repeat for the short edges.

2 Fold the linen in half lengthways and mark the center of the basket weave stripe about 2in/5cm from one end. Starting at the center fold, work the cross stitch pattern out to each side in turn with the flower thread. Work each cross stitch over two pairs of threads. *(see picture next column)*

On the hand towel, the herringbone pattern is worked in marking cross stitch. See page 105 for diagrams.

34 ◀

SHAKER

3 Cut a piece of linen 12 x 29½in/30 x 75cm with a basket weave stripe about 2in/5cm from each end. Fold the linen in half widthways and crease the fold. Work the three initials on the plain weave stripe, starting about 4in/10cm above the bottom crease and 3-4in/7.5-10cm from the right hand edge. Work each cross stitch over three threads.

4 Work the heart motif in the basket weave stripe below the stitched initials. Work the border design on the basket weave stripe 2in/5cm from each end of the fabric.

5 Fold the linen in half widthways and stitch the ⅜in/1cm side seams. Press the seams open.

6 Open out the corner and align the side seam over the bottom crease line. Tack and machine stitch across the corner about 1½in/4cm from the point. Zigzag across the corner close to the stitching and trim neatly.

7 Make up the lining in the same way, leaving a 2in/5cm gap in one side seam. Turn the lining through and tuck inside the linen bag. Pin the top edges, matching the seam lines. Machine stitch ⅜in/1cm from the raw edge.

8 Turn the bag and lining through the gap in the side seam and tuck the lining inside. Slip stitch the seam closed.

Press the cross stitched top edge of the toilet bag.

9 Machine stitch above and below the next basket weave stripe, about 2in/5cm down from the top edge. Thread the cord through the open weave of the linen and knot each end.

10 Pull the draw string to close the bag.

▶ 35

We think of Shaker furniture as being classic and timeless, but in their day it appeared impossibly plain and old-fashioned to the outside world. It is only because our style has moved away from chintz and flounces that we are able to appreciate its simple beauty. The Shaker style evolved from the early American Federal furniture that was in vogue towards the end of the 18th century. Whereas furniture styles in the outside world developed in tune with the trends of contemporary fashion, Shaker furniture was adapted to suit the constraints of communal living.

I have designed the furniture in this chapter to suit our lives today. They are all practical items that are entirely suited to their purpose, such as the versatile tray table, ideal for a late supper by the fire, or the simple dining bench, which allows us to squeeze in a few unexpected mealtime guests. The bench is in the style of true Shaker tradition, where utility is transcended by purity of line and form, allowing the beauty of the wood to be appreciated to the full. The towel rail too, is beautifully proportioned. It is simply made from pine, then "aged" with an antique stain. It has a useful shelf and a short peg rail for storing all the things you might need, and it could be adapted quite easily to fit the available space in a small kitchen or bathroom.

Space and convenience are key factors in the kitchen, where we need things to be close to hand when preparing food and cooking. Tin is an ideal material for the kitchen because it is fire-proof, and the utensil rack can safely be hung quite close to the stove so that the utensils are within easy reach. Tin has also been used to decorate the wooden pie safe which, like the other pieces in this

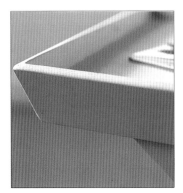

chapter, is designed along simple rectilinear lines, with the accent on function and form, rather than decoration. This is a useful little cupboard that can be used to keep baked pastries and pies crisp at room temperature, yet safe from flies. Although at first glance it seems more decorative than typical Shaker designs, it is very similar to the punched tin pie safes made by the Southern communities.

FURNITURE

utensil
rack

In the Shaker communities, lead-coated sheet iron was a commonly used material because it was cheap, plentiful, and easy to work. The workshops had patterns for all sorts of practical vessels and accessories such as milk pails, scoops, pitchers, colanders, and spatulas. The cut tin pieces were crimped and soldered together and were left "raw" or unpainted. Tin ware was sold throughout New England and New York State and it is now difficult to identify a genuine Shaker article.

This striking utensil rack is reminiscent of the triangular nail-studded frames used by the Shakers to dry bottles for use in their medicinal herb business. The tin plate is cut into strips and folded into shape. The folded edges are then punched at regular intervals with a chisel and steel punch. This is not intended as decoration but both strengthens the edge and helps to hold the shape; nevertheless, it adds to the visual appeal of the piece. The shaped tin strips are held together in a triangular shape with rivets which are inserted into pre-drilled holes.

Hang your most interesting – or most often used – metal utensils from the hooks, and store pastry cutters and other small gadgets on the shelf.

▶ 41

Most utensils have a hole in the handle, but if any of yours do not, just drill a generous hole and hang the utensil from one of the "s" hooks.

Invest in a pair of top quality tin snips to enable you to cut the clean straight lines that are essential to the success of this project. When you use the drill, start slowly to allow the drill bit to cut into the metal in a controlled fashion.

BASIC METALWORKING SKILLS
AND KNOWLEDGE OF POWER TOOLS
REQUIRED

MATERIALS
◆ 20 x 27½in/50 x 70cm sheet of 0.0116in/0.3mm tin plate
◆ Tin snips
◆ Length of scrap plywood
◆ Square
◆ Chisel
◆ Hammer
◆ Nail punch
◆ ¼in/5mm metal drill bit and drill
◆ ⅛in/3mm metal drill bit (optional)
◆ ¼in/5mm short rivets and rivet gun
◆ Seven wire "s" hooks
◆ Pencil and ruler
◆ Small block of wood
◆ Double-sided mirror tape
◆ Protective gloves

Finished size: about 25 x 26½ x 4in/ 64 x 67 x 10cm

1 Wearing gloves to protect your hands, cut a strip of tin plate 6 x 28in/15 x 70cm for the tray and two strips 4½ x 31½in/11.5cm x 80cm for the sides. *(see picture next column)*

If you prefer an "aged" look for your utensil rack you can give it a coat of metal lacquer.

42 ◀

2 Lay the tray piece on the plywood to protect the work surface. Mark a line ½in/1cm in from the front and the two sides. Mark a second line ⅝in/1.5cm further in. Position the chisel on the marked line and hammer to make a dent. Work along the lines to make a continuous groove.

3 Cut in from the front edge along the chiseled line furthest from each end as far as the inside corner point.

4 Fold over the front edge of the tin along the outer groove line and hammer flat from the wrong side.

5 Turn the tin over and use the hammer and chisel to make ½in/1cm lines, perpendicular to the edge, every ½in/1cm. Punch a dot in the center of each block. Fold the sides along the outer groove and decorate to match.

6 Mark the ½in/1cm and ⅝in/1.5cm lines along the back edge on the wrong side. Cut slits in the back edge to match the front slits. Fold the back edge over to the right side and hammer flat.

7 Fold up the front and back at 90° along the inner groove. Fold up the sides and tuck the end flaps inside the folded front and back edges. Check that all sides are at 90° and that the tray sits flat.

8 Mark ½in/1cm and ⅝in/1.5cm lines along one long side of the other tin strips. Mark a third line 1½in/4cm in from the other long side. Chisel along the lines to make a groove and bend over along the outer groove as before. Decorate both edges of the strips as before.

9 Fold each strip over at 90° along the remaining groove. Arrange the 3 pieces of tin in a triangle with the strips overlapping at the top. Check the side strips are level with the edge of the tray and then bend the top of the side strips into a neat point.

10 Using a block of wood for support, slowly drill two ¼in/5mm holes at each end of the back of the tray. Drill through the side strip and into the tray at the same time. Insert the rivets from the front and file the back if required.

11 Supporting the tin on a block of wood, drill a hole at the top of the triangle and 3 down each side strip, spacing them every 5in/12.5cm. Insert the rivets from the front. Hammer the ejected rivet rod back into the rivet from the front to remove the metal plug.

12 File a groove on the bottom edge of each rivet at the back. Insert the hooks into the rivet holes. Open out the hole with a ⅛in/3mm drill bit if necessary.

13 To hang, cut a block of wood to fit inside the top of the triangle. Secure the wood to the wall, and fix the rack over it with mirror tape.

tray table

One of the most famous Shaker sayings is "Beauty rests in Utility," arising from the belief that everything must be made for a purpose. The Shakers were constantly refining their designs to achieve a harmony between function and form. Their furniture designs were based on simple rectilinear forms stripped of vanity and excess.

The angled sides of this table top recall the gently sloping sides of the wooden carriers which the Shakers used to gather herbs from the fields, while the crossed legs are based on the workshop trestles which held bundles of broom handles. At first, most Shaker furniture was left unpainted, but in later years, much of the woodwork was painted red, blue or this pale, creamy yellow.

The Shakers were an egalitarian group and welcomed non-believers as guests, setting up extra tables in the dining rooms to accommodate them. This versatile table is collapsible and is specially designed so that it can be used at two different heights. When lowered, it can be used for a late TV dinner or for serving coffee, and when raised it is perfect for serving breakfast in bed.

The sides of the table are set at an angle, and the top edges planed smooth and then sanded to round them slightly.

This table is not a beginner's piece, although it is quite simple to make if you have the correct tools. Cut the table top carefully and plane it down to size so that it fits snugly. Seal the painted table with two coats of varnish to protect it from marking.

MATERIALS
- *3¼yd/3m of ½ x 3½in/12 x 90mm pine*
- *4⅓yd/4m of ¾ x 1¼in/20 x 32mm pine*
- *1yd/1m of ½ x 1¼in/12 x 34mm pine*
- *3yd/2.5m of ¾ x 1in/20 x 25mm pine*
- *8in/20cm of ¼ x ¾in/6 x 20mm pine*
- *3¼yd/3m of ⅛ x ½in/4 x 10mm pine strips*
- *21¼ x 37in/540 x 940mm sheet of ½in/12mm plywood*
- *39in/1m of ⅝in/15mm dowel*
- *Basic tool kit (see page 10)*
- *Two 5⁄16 x 2in/8 x 50mm carriage bolts, four washers and two nuts*
- *Four round-headed screws*
- *Band, fret or jigsaw*
- *Circular saw and plane*
- *Router and straight cutter*
- *Pale yellow reproduction milk paint*
- *Matte acrylic varnish and paintbrushes*
- *Cotton reel and pencil*

Finished size (at highest setting): 22⅜ x 38 x 30¼in/570 x 965 x 770mm

1 To make the sides of the table, cut the ½ x 3½in/12 x 90mm pine into two 21¼in/540mm and two 37in/940mm lengths. Mark ¾in/20mm in from the end along the bottom edge of each piece and draw a line from the mark to the top corner. Saw along the lines. *(see picture next column)*

2 Rout a ¼ x ¼in/6 x 6mm channel along each angled edge on the same side. Sand the rough edges. Drill and countersink two screw clearance holes on the right side of the long pieces, ¼in/6mm from the angled end.

3 Draw a line 1¾in/45mm below the top edge on the routed side of each side piece. Cut the pine strips to fit below the line, cutting the ends at an angle, ¼in/6mm from the routed edge. Glue the strips in place and pin until the glue dries.

4 Glue a short and long side piece together upside down. Drill a pilot hole through the countersunk holes and screw the joint together. Repeat on all four corners. Check that the corners are 90°, and lie the structure flat to dry overnight.

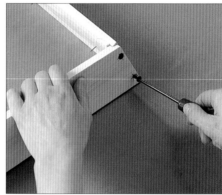

5 Fill the countersunk holes with wood filler and once dry, sand the filler and corner joints smooth. Plane along the top edge on each of the sides and sand to round off the edge.

6 Saw the plywood to fit inside the frame, allowing for the thickness of the plywood and the angle of the sides. Either use a circular saw set at the correct angle or plane the edges after cutting. Sand or plane the edges for a neat fit.

7 For the legs, saw the ¾ x 1¼in/20 x 32mm pine into four equal pieces. Use a cotton reel to draw a semicircle at each end.

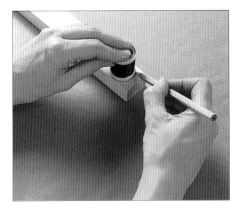

8 Saw the shape with a band, fret or jig-saw and sand smooth.

9 Mark the position of the dowel at one end of each leg and drill a ⅝in/15mm hole. Drill a clearance hole through the center of each leg for the carriage bolts.

10 Cut one piece of dowel 17in/430mm and another 19in/480mm long. Glue one dowel into the holes to join each pair of legs. Saw the ½ x 1¼in/12 x 34mm pine the same length as the dowels. Glue and tack a strap between each pair of legs, 8in/200mm from the end.
(see picture next column)

11 Cut three strips 16in/405mm and three 18in/455mm long from ¾ x 1in/20 x 25mm pine. Mark the center on the narrow side of each.

12 Drill and countersink a clearance hole in the center and one at each end of the six strips.

13 On the underside of the plywood base, draw a line 2¾in/70mm in from each short side and mark the center point. Place a short strip along the line, aligning the center points. Space the other two short strips ⅝in/15mm apart, so that a piece of dowel can slide between them.

14 Drill pilot holes into the plywood. Glue then screw the strips in place. Repeat at the other end to fix the longer strips.

15 Cut four equal lengths of ¼ x ¾in/6 x 20mm pine. Drill a screw hole at one end of each. Position two on each center strap, 4in/100mm from the end and drill pilot holes. Fix with round headed screws.
(see picture next column)

16 Rest the table sides on blocks and glue around the inside above the wood strips. Drop the plywood in place and weight it down overnight to dry.

17 Sand all the pieces with fine sandpaper. Paint the table top and legs. Finally, apply two coats of matte varnish.

18 Push the carriage bolts through the holes in the legs, inserting a washer between the legs and under the nut. If necessary, hammer the carriage bolt home before tightening the nut.

19 Turn the tray upside down and slot the leg dowels between the straps, choosing the low or high position. Lock in position and stand the table upright.

towel rail

Wood was plentiful in the newly settled lands where the Shakers lived and there were many talented cabinet makers and carpenters among the new converts – in fact, the Shakers became synonymous with consummate woodworking skills. The woodworkers made things according to the practical needs of the community, and wooden furniture and accessories were often specially designed to suit a particular purpose. The articles were made from plain undecorated wood, allowing the Brothers to concentrate on the proportion, balance, and craftsmanship of each piece. Over the years there were many innovations, such as the turned wooden pegs that were attached to wash stands and tables, or wherever they were thought useful. (Even large items, like chairs, were hung on the Shaker peg boards when not in use.)

This unusual unit is ideal for a small bathroom or kitchen. Like all Shaker furniture, it is plain and simple – and beautifully proportioned. With its towel rail, shelf, and row of pegs, you can "Provide places for all your things, so that you may know where to find them day or night," and so achieve tranquillity out of order.

The towel rail, whether made from old pine or new with an antique finish, is an ideal alternative to a typical bathroom cabinet, and makes a practical and charming storage unit in the kitchen.

The towel rail is the ideal project for re-using antique pine.
Make sure recycled pine is free of nails and have it dipped in a caustic bath to remove any old paint or varnish.
If you use new pine, as here, apply an antique pine stain to achieve the desired aged look.

MATERIALS
◆ 2¾yd/2.5m of ½ x 2¾in/12 x 70mm pine
◆ 27½in/700mm of ½ x 4¾in/12 x 120mm pine
◆ 20in/500mm of ¾ x 6in/20 x 150mm pine
◆ 20in/500mm of 15½in/10mm dowel
◆ 30in/750mm of ¾in/18mm dowel
◆ 8in/200mm of ¼in/6mm dowel
◆ Block of wood at least 1½in/40mm thick
◆ Basic tool kit (see page 10)
◆ 18mm wood drill bit
◆ Fret, band or jigsaw
◆ Antique pine stain
◆ Paintbrush and pencil
◆ Clear wax and soft rag

Finished size: 21 x 27½ x 5 ³/₁₆in/533 x 700 x 132mm

1 From the ½ x 2¾in/12 x 70mm pine, saw two 27½in/700mm lengths and two 21in/533mm lengths. Draw a quarter circle on the inside bottom edge of the two shorter pieces. Cut with a saw.

2 Lay the long pieces across the work bench 6¼in/160mm apart. Lay the side pieces on top at right angles over each end. Mark a diagonal line across each overlap. Mark, drill, and countersink two screw holes ⅝in/15mm from the edge on each diagonal.

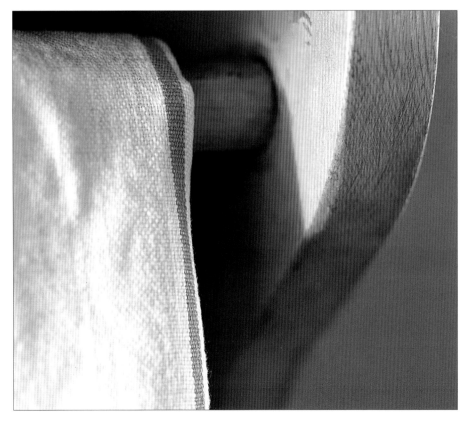

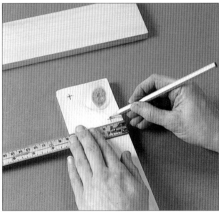

3 Reposition the wood and drill pilot holes through the horizontal pieces. Insert the screws. At the bottom of each upright, drill and countersink two screw holes for the shelf supports. The holes should be ⅝in/15mm in from the outside edge and 1in/25mm and 5in/125mm from the bottom curved edge.

The dowel fits into holes in the shelf support.

4 Turn the frame over and mark dowel holes in the opposite corners to the screws. Drill 1/4in/6mm holes right through the joints. Apply a little glue to each hole, then tap in a 1in/25mm piece of 1/4in/6mm dowel until it is flush.

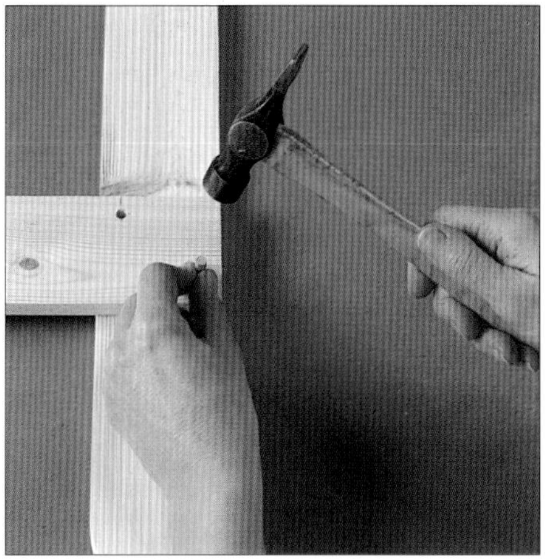

5 Enlarge the shelf support template at the back of the book and draw onto 3/4 x 6in/20 x 150mm pine with the grain running down the long straight edge. Saw along the curved edge. Use coarse sand paper to smooth the rough edges.

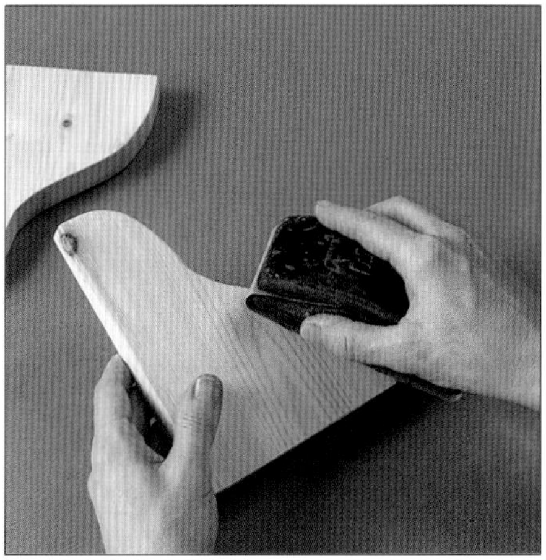

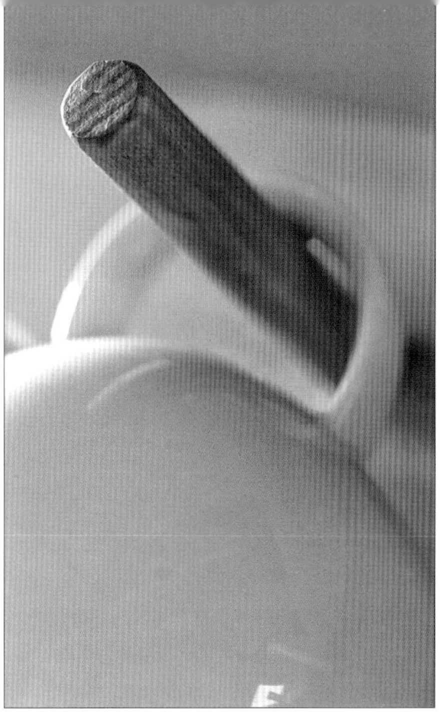

6 On the inside of each shelf support, mark the position of the center of the 3/4in/18mm dowel and drill a 3/4in/18mm shallow hole.

7 Sit the pre-cut piece of 1/2 x 43/4in/12 x 120mm pine for the shelf in position against the lower cross bar and mark two screw clearance holes 153/4in/400mm apart, 1/4in/6mm in from the back edge of the shelf. Drill and countersink the holes. Drill pilot holes through to the cross bar and glue then screw in place.

8 Position the shelf supports. Measure the distance between them and add the depth of the dowel holes. Cut a piece of 3/4in/18mm dowel to that length.

9 Hold the first shelf support in position with the frame upright and drill pilot holes through the clearance holes into the frame. Glue and screw in place. Insert the dowel and fit the second shelf support as before.

Each peg is hammered into a hole drilled at an angle with the aid of a jig, and the end of the peg is sanded to round it slightly.

10 In order to drill holes for the pegs at the same angle you will need to make a jig. Decide on the angle of the pegs and drill a 1/2in/10mm hole through the block of wood at that angle.

11 Mark the position of the four peg holes, evenly spaced along the top bar. Clamp the jig in position with the mark in the middle of the hole and the hole angled correctly. Put the drill bit into the hole and drill through the frame. Repeat for the other 3 holes.

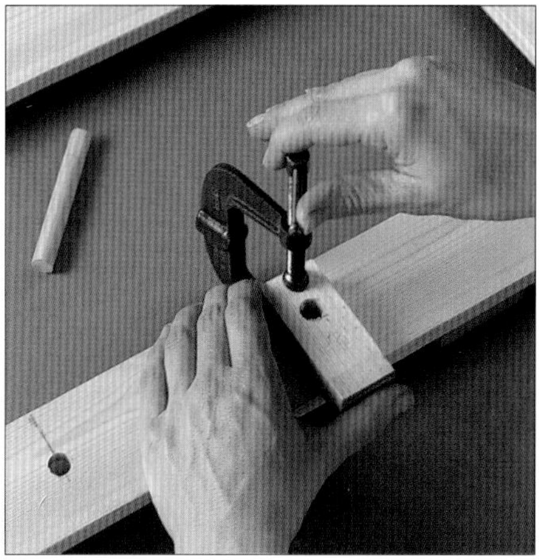

12 Saw the 1/2in/10mm dowel into four 4in/100mm lengths. Apply a little glue to the hole and hammer the dowels in. Sand the ends to round them off.

13 Sand all the edges to round them slightly and sand all the surfaces with fine sand paper. Apply antique stain and allow to dry. Apply several coats of clear wax and buff to a soft sheen.

dining bench

Both long and short benches were made by the Shaker communities for use in the meeting rooms and dining rooms. At mealtimes, the Brothers and Sisters sat on benches at long dining tables. The benches in the meeting rooms were moved and stacked to allow room for the ritual dances that were an important part of the group's beliefs. At the height of their success, the meeting rooms were busy places because non-believers were fascinated by the Shaker way of life and came to watch the dances, or "exercises" as they were known.

The benches therefore had to be plain and simple, easy to move and convenient to store. With no decorative embellishments to distract them, the carpenters were able to concentrate all their efforts on the shape and proportions of the benches and the way they fitted together.

Much of the Shaker furniture was made from the trees that grew locally. Hardwoods, such as birch and maple, were used but were usually stained with a red logwood dye to resemble mahogany. You can choose any hardwood for this bench, as long as the planks are wide enough to make the bench top.

The absence of fussy detail brings
the natural beauty of the
wood to the fore.

The legs on this dining bench have been cut away slightly along the bottom edge
to make four mini feet which allow the bench to stand square. Choose your favorite hardwood
or make the bench in pine and paint it the color of your choice.

BASIC WOODWORKING SKILLS
AND KNOWLEDGE OF POWER TOOLS
REQUIRED

MATERIALS
◆ *Three planks of ¾in/20mm hard-*
wood, each at least 10-12 x 48in/250-
300 x 1220mm
◆ *Basic tool kit (see page 10)*

◆ *Circular saw*
◆ *Router and straight cutter*
◆ *Plane*
◆ *Sanding sealer or varnish*
◆ *Paintbrush and pencil*
◆ *Clear wax and soft rag*

Finished size: 10-12 x 48 x 17¼in/
250-300 x 1220 x 440mm

1 Choose the best plank for the seat. Trim down the two long sides using a circular saw to make a plank 10-12in/250-300mm wide. Square off one end and measure a length of 48in/1220mm. Use the square to mark a line at 90° to the sides and saw to length.

2 Trim the long sides of the second plank to make it ½-¾in/10-20mm narrower than the seat. From this, saw two legs 16½in/420mm long. Mark 2in/50mm in from each side on the bottom of the legs. Rout a ¼in/6mm deep section along the bottom of the legs between the marks. Sand smooth the rough edges.

The bench has strong, clean lines and needs no further embellishment.

3 Cut two ¾ x 1¼in/20 x 30mm end supports ½in/10mm narrower than the legs. Plane a 45° angle along one long edge and around the ends. Sand the edge. On the narrow side, drill two screw clearance holes 1¼in/30mm from each end. On the wide side, drill holes 2in/50mm from the end.

4 Trim the third plank down the two long sides to make it 6in/150mm wide. Cut to a length of 37in/940mm.

5 At the top of the legs on the inside, draw the center line down about 6in/150mm using the square. Draw a second parallel line ⅜in/10mm to one side. Drill two screw clearance holes on the center line about ¾in/20mm and 4¾in/120mm from the top.

6 Turn the seat face down on a clean flat surface (a folded sheet will protect it). Stand the cross bar up in the center of the seat, an equal distance from each end. Mark its position down both sides.

7 Balance one of the legs against the crossbar, aligning the edge of the crossbar with the second line on the inside of the leg. Drill pilot holes for the screws through the pre-drilled and countersunk holes. Repeat for the second leg.

8 Lift the sections off and spread glue between the lines on the underside of the seat. Reposition the crossbar and spread glue down each end before screwing the legs in position.

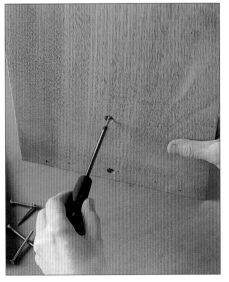

9 Spread glue on the flat sides of the end supports and press into position with the narrow side against the leg.

Check the supports are in the center of the legs before drilling pilot holes and screwing them in place. The screws going into the seat must not be too long.

10 Fill the screw holes with a matching wood filler. Stand the bench upright, weight the top and leave the bench to dry for 24 hours.

11 Sand down the wood filler and smooth any sharp edges. Sand all over with fine sandpaper, paying particular attention to the seat. Seal with sanding sealer or varnish. Once dry, rub in several coats of clear wax and buff to a soft sheen.

▶ 55

pie safe

The Shakers lived together in family groups of up to a hundred members. Family members were not necessarily related, but often did the same type of work, and so the families were named after the main occupation or by the proximity of their dwelling house to the meeting house. Every Sister in the family worked in the kitchens, usually on a four week rotation, and could make up to a thousand pies in that time. Fortunately the kitchens were spacious and equipped ahead of their time with ovens, arch kettles, and deep fryers.

This pie safe is a scaled-down version of the cupboard where the Sisters would store pies and pastries after baking. The mesh sides keep out flies and ensure that the pastry stays crisp (pastry put in a refrigerator tends to go soft).

The heart and tulips motif on the pie safe door was adapted from an inspirational painting, but it was a familiar motif all over colonial America. The motif is made from thin sheet metal which can be cut easily with scissors, and which readily accepts an embossed pattern. The corrugated edge on the heart was used on Shaker tin candle sconces, where it added strength with minimal decoration.

The patterns embossed on the foil hearts, leaves, and tulips add visual appeal and a measure of strength to the metal.

Metal foil is thinner than tin plate and can be cut easily with a pair of kitchen scissors.
You can use tin or pewter to give the same result. Pewter is more difficult to solder but can
be glued with an epoxy resin glue instead.

BASIC WOODWORKING SKILLS
AND KNOWLEDGE OF POWER TOOLS
REQUIRED

MATERIALS
◆ 4¹/₃yd/4m of ⁵/₈ x 1¹/₄in/15 x 34mm
pine
◆ 3²/₃yd/3.5m of ⁵/₁₆ x ³/₄in/8 x 18mm
pine
◆ 10¹/₂ x 14in/270 x 350mm of ¹/₄in/
6mm MDF
◆ Two pieces 12¹/₂ x 12³/₄in/316 x
325mm of ¹/₂in/12mm MDF
◆ Pewter foil
◆ Two sheets of Wireform square mesh
◆ Basic tool kit (see page 10)

◆ Band saw
◆ Veneer pins
◆ Fine galvanized wire
◆ Fine oxidized silver wire
◆ Two steel hinges
◆ Hook and eye catch
◆ Staple gun and staples
◆ Soldering iron and solder
◆ Epoxy resin glue
◆ Blue reproduction milk paint
◆ Paintbrush
◆ Embossing tool and craft scissors
◆ Mouse pad

Finished size: 12¹/₂ x 12³/₄ x 15in/316 x
325mm x 380mm

1 Measure and saw six *12in/300mm*
and six *14in/350mm* lengths of ⁵/₈ x
1¹/₄in/15 x 34mm pine. Cut a ⁵/₁₆ x
1¹/₄in/7 x 34mm section from each end
of the strips, on the same side. Glue
one short and one long piece together
and check that the corner is 90°. Make
up the other five corners and clamp
them one on top of the other overnight
until the glue sets.

2 Glue the corner sections together to
make three frames, checking again that
the corners are 90° before clamping.
Once dry, fill in any gaps with wood
filler and sand smooth any rough edges.

3 From the narrow pine, saw two strips
11³/₄in/294mm long and ten *10¹/₂in/
270mm* long. Make the shelf by gluing
and pinning 10 evenly spaced cross
strips to the narrow edge of the side

Use an embossing tool to create the patterns.

pieces. Knock the pins with a hammer to just below the surface and fill the holes with wood filler.

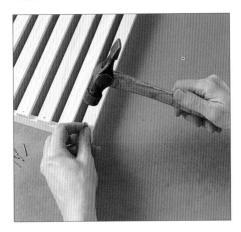

4 Build up the pie safe and glue the edges, insetting the thin MDF panel between the sides at the back. Use the shelf to support the front edge (temporarily). Tape the pieces together and check that all corners are 90°.

5 Glue and nail the top in place, then turn the pie safe over and nail the base in position. Punch the nails below the surface and fill with wood filler. Allow to dry for 24 hours.

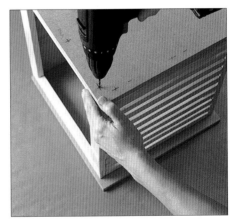

6 Give the pie safe and shelf a final sand before applying two coats of paint.

7 Staple the mesh inside the door and side panels. Position the shelf half way up the cupboard and hammer pins in at the front and back to hold it in position.

8 Trace the template at the back of the book. Draw around each shape on the pewter foil using the embossing tool. Cut the shapes out.

9 Lay them one by one on the reverse side of a mouse pad and mark a pattern onto the foil with the embossing tool.

10 Cut lengths of galvanized wire and solder to the back of the pewter shapes. Take great care as the pewter will melt if it touches the soldering iron. You can use glue instead.

11 Arrange the tulips and leaves and solder the stems together. Trim the ends of the wire and solder or glue to the back of the heart. Glue the heart to the door mesh and fix the tulip and leaf stems with fine oxidized silver wire ties trimmed neatly on the inside.

12 To finish, fix the hinges to the left side of the door and fix a hook and eye catch to the middle of the right side.

containers

"You must not lose one moment of time for you have none to spare." This maxim, attributed to the Shaker founder, Mother Ann Lee, is as relevant to our busy lifestyle as it was to the Shaker communities whose members spent their days in a strict routine of work and worship. Believers were encouraged to lead ordered lives and to put things back in the right place so that others could use them. Today, when one family member is arriving just as another goes out, and spare time seems to belong to the past, it is increasingly important to maintain a measure of order and neatness. Think how much time we would save if we didn't have to search the house for that elusive sock, button or key!

It makes style sense to hide clutter in containers which will complement and enhance the furnishings and the ambience of the room. Whereas a plastic box would look unsightly on the coffee table, a finely made oval wooden box would not. The Shaker box is not air-tight but is made in such a way that the lid fits snugly. It can therefore be used to store all manner of dry goods from herbs and spices to buttons, nails, and screws. The candle box is designed to hold a dozen tall candles, with little drawers for matches or tea lights, but it would not look out of place stood upright on a desk and filled with pens and pencils. Baskets, too, are useful containers, but for an uncluttered look, more thought has to be given to what you put in them. An open weave basket, such as the one described, can achieve an almost sculptural look when filled with fruit or a clutch of eggs.

A simple laundry bag tied to a wooden towel rail could be just the thing to get dirty clothing off the bathroom floor. In keeping with the Shaker principle "That is best which works best," the linen bag I have designed retains its shape even when full, and is easily emptied using the simple tie fastening on the back.

The Shakers used peg boards to hang chairs and equipment out of the way when they were not in use, as many as 5000 pegs being available in the 50 rooms in Hancock, Massachusetts, for example. My tree of life peg board is unashamedly decorative, yet completely practical. It can be used to store keys or small tools, so that every family member knows where to find them.

CONTAINERS

w o v e n   b a s k e t

The Shakers made many different types of basket and were renowned for the quality of their basketry. At first, when they made only heavyweight utility baskets, basketry was men's work, but with the shift to "fancy," specialist designs, the Sisters became involved, and basket-making became important winter work for all.

Shaker baskets were made from thin oak and ash splint prepared in the fall. This is not readily available, so lapping cane, sold by the pound/half kilogram, has been used to achieve a similar effect. This unusual hexagon weave basket was made to hold wheels of cheese in order to drain off the whey. The basket looks complicated but is quite simple to make as no special equipment is required, apart from a few clothes pins, and the cane does not need extensive pre-soaking.

The width of the cane you use will determine the size of the hexagons and the finished basket. The basket shown is about 10in/25cm in diameter.

The hexagonal pattern of the open weave is sturdy enough to support a dozen eggs, yet fine enough to create an almost sculptural effect.

Although it looks quite complex, the basket is simple to make as there are few techniques to master. The cane does not need lengthy soaking but remember to dry out thoroughly any cane left over at the end of each session.

1 Dip all the cane in cold water and put it directly into the bag to keep it damp.

2 Using the 23¾in/60cm lengths of lapping cane, lay one piece (A) horizontally on a flat surface. Weave in two more lengths (B and C) diagonally to form an interlocking triangle in the center of the 3 pieces of cane. Lock A, B, and C together tightly, making sure that B (in the right hand) runs over the top of C.

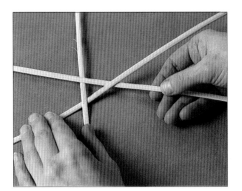

3 Continue adding diagonal lengths (B and C) on either side of the triangle until there are 16 diagonal pieces. Make sure all the B lengths cross over the C lengths, and under A. Lock the triangles together tightly and check that all the angles of the triangles are 60°.

4 Begin weaving the second horizontal A length, lifting up the B and C lengths as you come to them. Weave the A length under all the C lengths and over all the B lengths and lock the B and C lengths together above the horizontal A length.

5 You will now have seven hexagonal spaces. Adjust the cane so that all the spaces are exactly the same size and shape.

6 Weave in the last six horizontal A lengths, three above and three below the first two. Each time, weave over two diagonal lengths less than before, to make a large hexagon that will form the base of the basket.

7 Fix a clothes pin to each corner of the hexagon to hold it securely. Work away from your body around the outside of the basket to weave the sides.

8 Starting in the center of one side of the hexagon, bend two lengths up and pin the end of a coil of cane in place to form a triangle. Bending up the lengths as you go, weave in front and behind the lengths to form the sides. Lock the lengths together above the coil of cane to form the hexagonal spaces.

9 At each corner the space will be five-sided, not six as before. Pin the crossed cane above the pentagon with clothes pins to hold the shape. Weave all the way around in this way, overlapping the end by at least two triangles. Trim the excess cane.

10 Weave three more rows, making sure that all the hexagons are the same shape and size. After the first row, the basket sides should be vertical.

11 Spray the basket with water to re-dampen the cane. Bend all the diagonal lengths alternately to the inside and outside over the top of the last horizontal coil and pin them in place with clothes pins.

12 Pin one piece of the flat band cane around the inside rim of the basket and one on the outside. Overlap the ends of each piece.

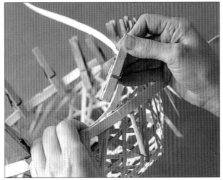

13 Anchor the end of a well-dampened coil of cane between the pieces of flat band cane. Wrap the cane over the rim of the basket and back through each hexagon in turn to give a line of slanting stitches. Pull the cane tight as you go. (*see picture next column*)

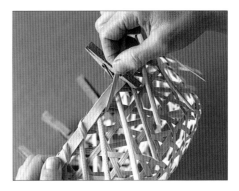

14 When you reach the start again, go back in the opposite direction to make a second row of stitches slanting the other way. Trim the end and tuck into the flat band cane rim to secure.

15 Trim off all the ends of the cane close to the rim and leave the basket to dry away from direct heat. Seal the cane with varnish or treat with teak oil.

The rim is strengthened with flat band cane.

▶ 67

tree of life peg board

The Tree of Life is a symbol common to arts and crafts all over the world. In the Middle East, rugs woven with the design are hung upside down so that the roots are nearer to heaven. It is likely that the Tree of Life was introduced to America through the widespread imports from the East India Company, and it appears as a symbol of life and love in many inspirational drawings.

The design for this wirework Tree of Life is based on a painting by Hannah Cohoon, a Sister from the Church family in Hancock, Massachusetts. Her paintings were unusual because they were inscribed with her name and featured a single scene, boldly painted using a thick tempera rather than the more usual watercolor.

The galvanized wire used for the branches and fruit on the tree is available from craft or hardware stores. It should be thin enough to coil with pliers but thick enough to hold its shape. The silver jewelry wire used to make the leaves and wrap the stems is very shiny and should be oxidized.

The peg board is hung from two "D" rings fixed to the back, allowing the canopy of the wirework Tree of Life to float freely above.

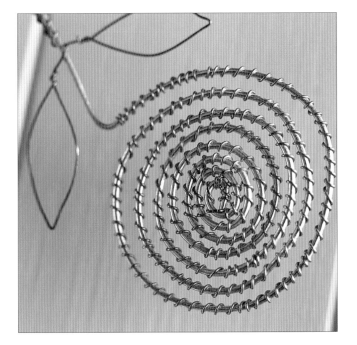

Since the wire is springy, protect your eyes with safety goggles and stick a tab of masking tape over the cut end of each wire before you begin. Use potassium sulfate crystals to give an "antiqued" look. Dried egg or bleach works just as well, though more slowly.

MATERIALS
◆ 0.078in/2mm galvanized wire
◆ 0.025in/0.65mm silver wire
◆ 0.025in/0.65mm copper wire
◆ 12in/300mm of ½in/12mm pine
◆ Potassium sulfate crystals
◆ Four 1in/2.5cm bun handles
◆ Small parallel pliers
◆ Wire cutters
◆ Fret, band or jigsaw
◆ Basic tool kit (see page 10)
◆ Round file
◆ Staple gun and staples
◆ Two "D" rings
◆ Off-white reproduction milk paint
◆ Matte acrylic varnish
◆ Paintbrushes
◆ Safety goggles

Finished size (peg board): 4 x 13in/100 x 330mm

1 Cut a 20in/50cm length of galvanized wire and make a loop at one end. Secure the end of the copper wire to the loop and wrap it tightly round the galvanized wire to form open twists. *(see picture next column)*

Each piece of galvanized wire is wrapped in silver wire and coiled seven or eight times to make the fruit.

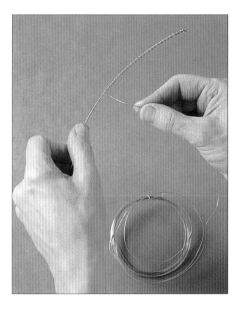

2 Hold the loop with the pliers and begin to coil the wrapped wire. After the first few turns, hold the coil flat between the blades and bend the wire around. Continue to wrap the galvanized wire as required and keep coiling it around until it is 2in/5cm across.

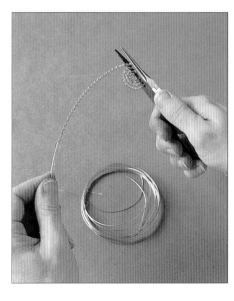

3 Make 14 coiled stems using the enlarged template at the back of the book as a guide and bending the stems into soft curves.

4 Bend a 20in/50cm length of silver wire 2in/5cm from the end and open it out to form a leaf shape. Twist the end of the wire around the stem. Bend the wire to make another leaf on either side and twist the end around the stem to secure.

5 Make 15 triple leaves and 4 single leaves. Check their positions on the template and lift the stem up so that you can wrap the end of the silver wire down the stem. Continue adding the leaves in this way to complete the tree.

6 Crush a crystal of potassium sulfate in a little water and brush the solution over the silver wire. This causes the silver to oxidize, lose its shine and turn shades of tortoiseshell.

7 Trace the wood template and draw the shape on the pine. Saw along the curved line. Sand the edges using coarse sand paper. File a central groove at the top on the back to allow the tree stem to lie fairly flat.

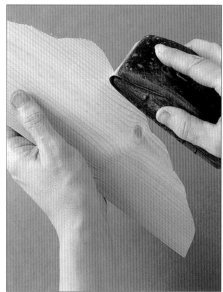

8 Drill four evenly spaced holes for the handles. Glue then screw on the handles. Apply two coats of paint to the wood and allow to dry. Sand the edges and handle tops to distress the paint. Varnish the wood.

9 Fan out the wires below the wrapped silver wire at the base of the stem. Turn the tree over. With the handles underneath and hanging over the edge of the work surface, position the wire stem on the base. Staple the fan of wires to the wood and trim the ends.

10 Screw two "D" rings onto the back of the base and hang the peg board on the wall.

shaker box

Shaker boxes are made in carefully graded sizes so that they can be stacked or stored one inside the other. They were originally made from thin sheets of maple or birch veneer, but birch plywood is more suitable for a beginner. The layers of ply have the grain going in alternate directions so the wood is less likely to split during construction. Use special water and boil proof (WBP) plywood so that it can be immersed in hot water before bending.

When these boxes are made on a commercial scale, the bands are soaked in custom-made copper tanks, but you can use a fish kettle or similar receptacle. The hot, wet band is bent to shape round an oval forming block. You can make a forming block in the size of your choice from MDF or thick plywood.

Shaker boxes are not difficult to make, provided you have the correct tools, such as a band saw for cutting the basic shapes, and a disc sander to shape the oval top and base for a perfect fit. And remember, one Shaker box is never enough, so keep the oval shapers and forming block for future use!

▶ 73

The copper tacks are hammered into marked and pre-drilled holes in the birch ply, and are an attractive detail clearly visible even after the box has been painted.

Make a forming block by gluing together ovals of thick plywood or MDF oversize and smoothing the sides against a disc sander. Glue this to a larger oval base ready for use. You must use the correct grade of birch ply (available from timber suppliers) to ensure success.

BASIC WOODWORKING SKILLS
AND KNOWLEDGE OF POWER TOOLS
REQUIRED

MATERIALS

◆ 1/4in/6mm and 1/16in/1.5mm birch ply, grade 111, Finnish, WBP (water and boil proof)
◆ Band saw, belt sander, disc sander
◆ 1/16in/1.5mm and 5/64in/2mm drill bits and drill
◆ 4in/100mm high forming block (use the template at the back of the book)
◆ Heavy-duty craft knife and cutting mat
◆ Block of wood
◆ Copper tacks
◆ Sandpaper
◆ Fish kettle or similar container
◆ Oval shapers
◆ Anvil – a fixed metal tube is fine
◆ Tack hammer
◆ Tooth picks
◆ Reproduction milk paint
◆ Wax or matte acrylic varnish
◆ Paintbrushes and pencil

Finished size: about 3-3/4 x 6 x 2-1/4in/ 95 x 150 x 57mm

1 Make templates for the side and lid bands using the ones at the back of the book. The length of the side band is 19in/483mm and the lid band, 19-15/16in/490mm. Lay the templates on the 1/16in/1.5mm birch ply with the grain running lengthways. Mark the outline and the position of the tacks. Cut out with the band saw.

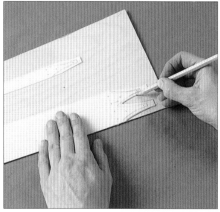

2 Feather the last 3/4-1-1/4in/20-30mm at the square end of the strips. This involves sanding the birch ply to make it gradually thinner towards the end. A belt sander gives the best results.

3 Soak the swallowtail end of the side band in a fish kettle of scalding hot water for a few minutes and lay on the cutting mat, feathered end up. To bevel the swallowtail ends, hold the craft knife at a 10° angle and cut a gentle gothic arch, making the tips of the tails no more than 1/4in/6mm wide. Bevel the tips. Drill the tack holes with the finer drill bit.

4 Soak the whole side band in very hot water for 10 minutes. Have the forming block and anvil ready. Remove the band and wrap it, beveled edge out, round the block. The main tack line should be central on the side of the block. Mark the overlap with a pencil.

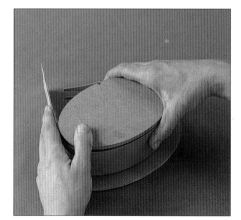

5 Take the band off the block and realign the pencil marks. Hold the swallowtails securely and hammer copper tacks into the pre-drilled holes. Hammer against the anvil so that they clinch inside the plywood.

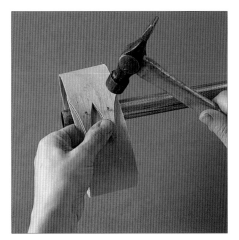

6 Insert the oval shapers in the top and base of the box, keeping the main tack line on the center mark.

7 Do not force them into position. The lid band is made in the same way as the side band. Wrap around the box, mark the overlap and insert the tacks. Replace on the top of the box and leave to dry, away from direct heat, for 2 days.

8 Sand the inside of the box and lid bands. Draw around the inside of the box and lid bands to make a template for the top and base. Using a band saw, cut the shapes out just outside the line from ¼in/6mm birch ply with the grain running lengthways.

9 Smooth the sides exactly down to the line with a disc sander. Set the sander at an angle of 4° to bevel the edges for a tight fit.

10 With the swallowtails facing to the left, push the base into the box. Fit the lid top with the swallowtails facing to the right. Sand the top and base of the box flush with the bands.

11 Set the drill on its side with a ¹⁄₁₆in/1.5mm drill bit and clamp in position. Rest the box on a block of wood and drill holes ⅛in/3mm above the block at 2in/5cm intervals around the base. Repeat for the lid.

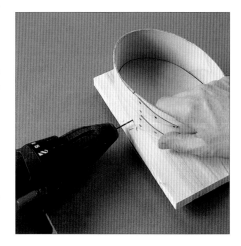

12 Tap half tooth picks into the holes, snip off the ends and sand flush.

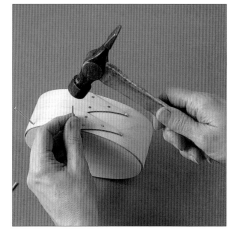

13 Paint the boxes and wax or varnish to seal the surface. Try antique gold, deep red or uniform blue shown in the picture at the top of the opposite page. If you intend to store food in the box, leave the inside unpainted.

candle box

The decorative ornaments that we have in our homes had no place in the Shaker dwellings. Instead, they made useful objects – such as this wooden candle box – which could be hung from peg boards when not in use. Originally all wooden objects in the Shaker community were made from unpainted wood, but in later years, colors such as ochre yellow, blue and this deep burgundy were used in moderation and became a tradition.

In order to achieve the delicate appearance associated with Shaker woodwork, I chose to make the candle box from MDF. This is a smooth, easily-cut material that is unaffected by the changes in humidity and temperature in a modern home. Unlike thin hardwood or pine, it will not distort with time.

The box is made by cutting the pieces out with a saw and gluing them together. The assembly of the drawers requires some precision, but is not difficult, and you will find that rubbing a candle along the bases will help them glide in and out more easily. The handles are made from lengths of hemp string that are knotted on the inside.

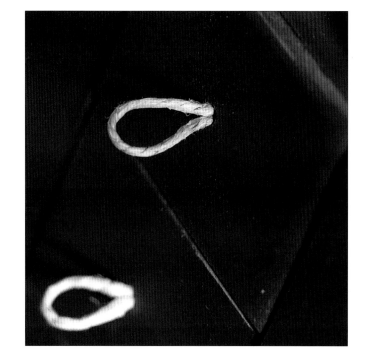

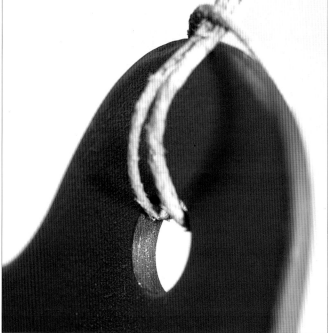

The compartments are designed to each hold six ¾in/2cm candles.
Since MDF contains resin, its sawdust is toxic and you must wear a dust mask when making the box.
Birch ply is a suitable alternative.

MATERIALS
◆ *20 x 24in/500 x 610mm of ¼in/ 6mm MDF*
◆ *Band or jigsaw*
◆ *Basic tool kit (see page 10)*
◆ *Sanding sealer*
◆ *Sponge sanding pad*
◆ *Dark red matte acrylic paint*
◆ *Matte acrylic varnish*
◆ *Paintbrushes*
◆ *Hemp string*
◆ *Steel wool*

Finished size: 10½ x 12¼ x 2½in/270 x 310 x 62mm

1 Enlarge the template at the back of the book for the back panel and transfer the outline to the MDF. Cut out using a band or jigsaw fitted with a narrow blade. Mark the position of the hole in the handle and drill a large hole.

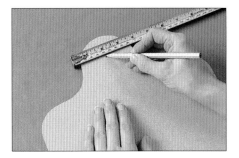

2 Cut the MDF for the candle holders and drawers and label each piece.

Base: 2½ x 10½in/62 x 270mm; 4 sides: 2 x 5¾in/50 x 144mm; 3 drawer fronts: 2 x 3in/50 x 80mm; 2 box fronts: 3¾ x 6in/95 x 150mm; drawer top and 2 dividers: 2 x 3in/50 x 80mm; 6 drawer sides: 1½ x 1¾in/38 x 44mm; 3 drawer backs: 1½ x 2¾in/ 38 x 68mm.

3 Glue the back edges of the side panels and the box fronts. Tape in position on the back panel. Check the pieces are square. Then weight and leave to dry for 24 hours.

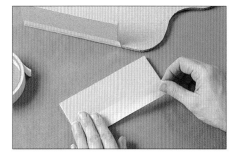

4 Glue the drawer top and dividers 1⅜in/36mm apart inside the candle box. Tape in position. Glue and tape the base of the box in place.

5 Drill a ⅛in/3mm hole in the center of each drawer front. Glue then tape the drawer pieces together upside down so that the side and back panels are flush with the top. Check the corners are square and leave to dry for 24 hours.

6 Sand the edges of the candle box and drawer fronts. Brush the entire box with a sanding sealer and leave to dry. Rub lightly with a fine sanding pad.

7 Paint the candle box with two coats of paint. Leave to dry thoroughly and then distress the edges with steel wool. Coat with varnish.

8 Thread a loop of string through the hole in each drawer front and tie a knot inside the drawer. Trim the excess string on the inside.

9 Cut another length of hemp string to hang the candle box. Double it over to make a loop and knot the ends securely. Push the loop through the large hole at the top of the candle box and catch the knotted end through it.

laundry bag

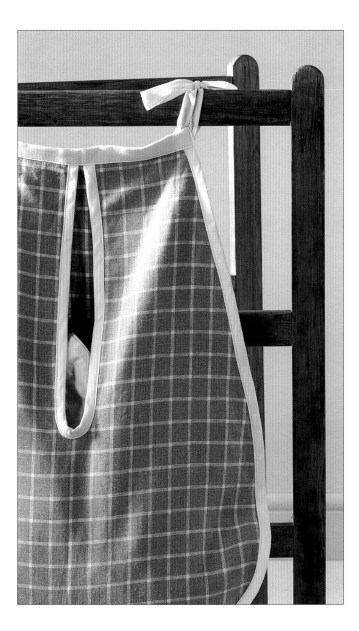

Despite evolving slightly over the years, Shaker clothes were essentially styled on the clothes the original members wore at the end of the 18th Century, so that, by the end of the 19th Century, their style of dress seemed quaint. As was the custom of the time, the women wore separate "pockets" hidden under the top skirt and tied at the waist which were used to hold odds and ends. Access to them was via small slits in the sides of the top skirt. The pockets did not need to match the outer garment and were therefore often made from pieced patchwork strips to use up scraps of fabric and avoid waste.

This laundry bag was designed to echo the shape of these pockets and is large enough to hold a substantial amount of washing. It is made from a simple check linen that is similar to the fabric the Shakers would have used themselves. The Shakers wove quantities of plain tape to make the traditional seat covers and may well have used fabric tape to tie their pockets in place.

The raw edges of the laundry bag are neatly bound with contrasting binding, which not only looks attractive, but helps maintain the shape of the bag as it fills.

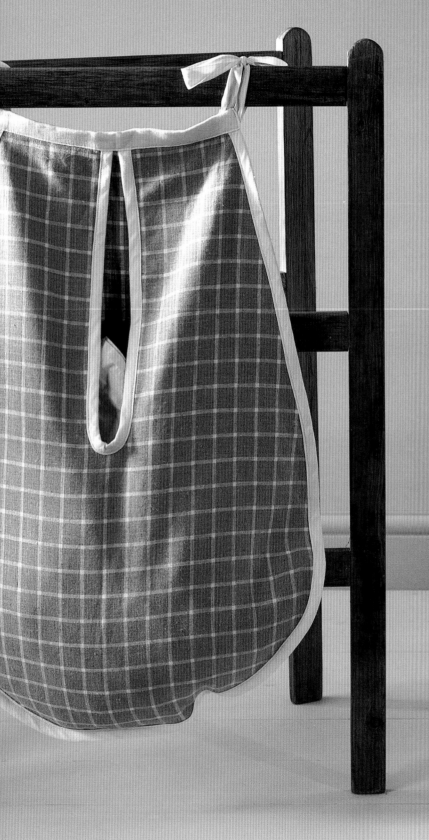

This capacious laundry bag has a tie fastening on the back
so that you can empty the contents quickly. Sew the ends of the twill tapes on securely
in a square formation to give them extra strength.

MATERIALS
◆ 1yd/1m check Cork linen
◆ 1/2 yd/0.5m white linen
◆ 4yd/3.5m white twill tape
◆ Sewing kit and sewing machine
◆ Ruler, pencil and paper

Finished size (at widest point): about
21 x 30in/53 x 75cm

1 Enlarge the template at the back of the book. For the front, fold the Cork linen down the center of a white line and pin the template along the fold. Cut out the slot and then the shape. For the back, ignore the slot and place the long line 5/8 in/1.5cm from the selvages. Cut around the curved edge only.

2 To make the back opening, pin the back pieces right sides together along the selvages and machine down 15in/38cm. Reverse stitch at the end to strengthen.

The front of the bag has an opening for inserting the laundry.

3 Turn under the remaining selvage seam allowance and machine two parallel rows 1/4in/6mm apart to secure the hem, and top stitch. Sew 2 pairs of 10in/25cm pieces of twill tape to opposite edges, about 4in/10cm apart.

4 Position the ruler at 45° across the corner of the white linen. Draw lines 2 1/2in/6.5cm apart and cut enough strips to fit around the edge of the slot and the curved edge of the bag.

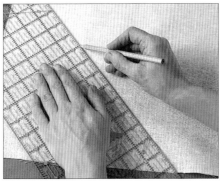

5 To join the strips, overlap the ends at 90° so that the points protrude 1/4in/6mm on each side. Stitch across and press the seam open. Cut off the points. Press the strip to remove the stretch.

6 Turn under 5/8in/1.5cm on both edges of the binding and, working on the right side of the bag, pin the binding over the raw edge of the slot, easing it neatly around the bottom curve. Tack, then machine stitch from the right side, securing both sides of the binding as you go. (see picture next column)

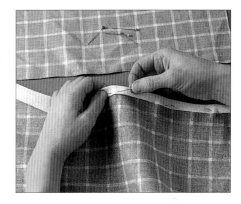

7 With wrong sides facing, pin and tack the front and back together. Pin the binding around the curved edge only and tack and stitch from the front as before.

8 Pin the center of two 36in/90cm strips of twill tape to each end of the top. Cut a 4 x 11in/10 x 28cm strip of white linen on the straight grain. Turn under 5/8in/1.5cm on both edges and pin over the raw top edge. Trim and tuck in the ends of the binding. Tack and sew from the right side, as before.

▶ 81

▶ 83

It is the accessories which breathe life into a home, making it less bare and more inviting. While not strictly essential, they fill the empty space on a wall, add a touch of color to a room or brighten up a dull corner. These little "extras" help to make life more comfortable – and a great deal more interesting. For this chapter, I have designed five accessories, each of which can be used to add a touch of Shaker style to your home.

Although the Shakers would not tolerate anything that had no use – "Whatever is fashioned let it be plain and simple and for the good" – they were practical people and would rather make a rug for the bare floor than have cold feet in winter. They made several types of rag rug, but the hooked rug was perhaps the most common. The hooked rug is made with strips of recycled wool fabric (rather than cotton), so that it doesn't flatten with use, and the method is adaptable to any size or shape. The other woolen accessory I have included is a knitted throw, worked in two basic stitches and simple enough for the beginner. The throw can be draped over the couch to add textural interest, or used as an extra blanket.

There is nothing quite as cozy or comforting as the warm, flickering light from lots of candles. The Shakers used many different styles of candle holders or sconces, but most were made from tin as it was cheap, plentiful and, most importantly, fire-proof. A store-bought baking tin makes an ideal basis for the candle sconce, and you could make a whole assortment to hang around your home.

Wood was by far the most common material used in the Shaker communities and was used to make furniture as well as accessories. At first, wood was left "raw," even varnish being a hotly-debated ethical issue, but as the years went by, it became more acceptable to varnish – and even paint – the "movables," as they were known. The Shakers relied on clocks and notice boards to maintain their strict routine. The wall clock, painted in a serene Shaker color, is reminiscent of the style of the Southern communities, while the charming alphabet board, based on the Shaker school room boards, would be an asset to family communication in any busy home.

ACCESSORIES

wall clock

There were clock makers in each of the communities. Some made only the mechanisms, leaving the cases to the carpenters, while others, like Isaac Newton Youngs, made complete clocks. Isaac Newton Youngs belonged to the Church family in New Lebanon, New York. He wrote a daily journal describing in great detail the community life that became a standard for other believers. Initially, while the communities were being established, there was not much time for clock making, but as the Shakers prospered, members were keen to have a clock of their own. In 1856 Isaac wrote "... I don't see there is any stopping until we get a clock in every room and shop."

The case of this clock is styled on clocks made in Pleasant Hill and South Union, Kentucky. Much of the furniture in these Southern communities showed a vernacular influence, with bold projecting moldings that were quite alien to the New England communities. Most of the Shaker clocks displayed Roman numerals. The face of this clock was aged using crackle varnish. Raw umber oil paint was then applied to the cracked surface to soften the stark white and blend the edges into the green surround.

The delicate flange around the top of this clock has been cut down from a piece of architrave. The joints were filled carefully and sanded down to make the top completely flat. "Age" the clock face before fitting it into the door.

MATERIALS
◆ 4¹⁄₃yd/4m of ⁵⁄₈ x 1¹⁄₄in/15 x 34mm pine
◆ 1²⁄₃yd/1.5m of ³⁄₄ x 6in/20 x 150mm pine
◆ 39in/1m of ⁵⁄₈in/15mm architrave

◆ 20 x 24in/500 x 610mm of ¹⁄₄in/6mm MDF
◆ 1in/2.5cm bun handle
◆ 6in/15cm white clock face
◆ Clock mechanism and hands
◆ Basic tool kit (see page 10)
◆ Band saw and miter saw
◆ Router
◆ Two steel hinges
◆ Door catch

◆ Green reproduction milk paint
◆ Aging varnish and crackle varnish
◆ Burnt umber oil paint
◆ Matte acrylic varnish
◆ Paintbrushes

Finished size (excluding flange): 10¹⁄₂ x 16³⁄₄ x 6¹⁄₂in/270 x 425 x 165mm

1 Mark and saw two 10¹⁄₂in/270mm and two 16¹⁄₂in/420mm lengths of ⁵⁄₈ x 1¹⁄₄in/15 x 34mm pine. Cut a ⁵⁄₁₆ x 1¹⁄₄in/7 x 34mm section from each end of the lengths, on the same side. Glue one short and one long piece together. Make up the other corner. Check that the corners are 90°, then clamp in position overnight until the glue sets.

The clock face is "aged" with aging varnish, then crackle varnish, and finally a touch of burnt umber paint to accentuate the cracks.

2 Glue the corner sections together to make the door frame, checking that the corners are 90° before clamping. Once dry, fill in any gaps with wood filler and sand smooth any rough edges.

3 Rout a ¼in/6mm channel around the inside edge of the door frame on the wrong side. Cut a piece of MDF to fit. Mark the center of the MDF 5in/130mm down from the top and drill a ½in/10mm hole. Glue the MDF in place.

4 Saw the ¾ x 6in/20 x 150mm pine into two 10½in/270mm pieces and two 16in/405mm pieces. Rout a ½ x ¾in/10 x 20mm section from both ends of each short piece.

5 Assemble the clock face so that the sides fit into the cut out section and mark the inside back edge of each piece. Rout a ¼in/6mm channel along each marked edge.

6 Trim ⅝in/15mm from the square edge of the architrave. Cut a piece of

the square section to fit the width of the clock case. Glue and pin across the top at the front.

7 Glue the case sections together. Mark and drill pilot holes, then nail on first the top and then the base. Sink the nails below the surface with a punch. Fill the holes with wood filler.

8 Cut a piece of MDF to fit the recess and glue in place. Check that the MDF is square before weighting and leaving to dry for 24 hours.

9 Hold the architrave in front of the added square section and mark the inside measurement of the miter. Cut the angle using a miter saw. Cut miters on two other pieces of architrave and trim the square ends to length.

10 Glue the edges of the mitered corners and glue the architrave to the top of the clock case, first to the piece of square section at the front, and then to the sides. *(see picture next column)*

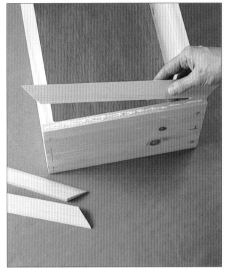

11 Use masking tape to hold the architrave flush with the top edge, and tape the two mitered corners. Leave for 24 hours to allow the glue to dry.

12 Fill any gaps with wood filler. When dry, sand the top of the clock case and door frame, then rub all over with fine sand paper. Drill a hole on the door frame and screw on the handle.

13 Apply two coats of paint and a coat of varnish. Fix the hinges to the door and fit the door catch on the inside.

14 Apply a thin, even coat of aging varnish to the clock face. Leave for at least an hour until almost touch dry. Apply a coat of crackle varnish. Smooth carefully with your finger and leave to dry over-night.

15 Rub a dab of oil paint into the cracks. Polish off the excess with a soft cloth. Fit the clock and mechanism according to the manufacturer's instructions.

hooked rug

Although their furniture and surroundings appeared austere, the Shakers lived in relative comfort, with specially designed cast iron stoves to heat the dwelling houses and workshops. The Shaker laws which covered most aspects of community life were essentially practical and, amongst other things, advocated the use of rugs and floor coverings to cover the wooden floors. Each Brother and Sister had a small hooked, braided or knitted rug beside their bed, and longer woven carpets were used in other parts of the building.

The rugs were often made from the fabric of old and worn out clothes, cut into strips. The strips were either pushed through heavy burlap to produce a pile, or plaited into long braids that were coiled and stitched in place. The laws banned figurative design but made no other restrictions, with the result that the rugs are the most colorful of the Shaker textiles.

The red hearts on this hooked rug recall the traditional color of the "Dorothy cloaks" that were woven from woolen broadcloth and worn by the Sisters in winter. The black border is typical, although Shaker hooked rugs usually also had a braid border around the outside.

Plan the color scheme of your rug carefully before you begin, and, for maximum effect, make sure the motif is in clear contrast to the background color.

Collect wool fabric for this hooked rug by searching for old blankets
and suitable garments in charity shops. Here the same tweed fabric has been dyed in several
different shades to make the backgrounds for the hearts.

MATERIALS
- ¾yd x 1yd/0.75 x 1m burlap
- Assorted wool fabric cut into ¼in/ 6mm strips
- Wide twill tape, pre-washed and dyed to match border fabric
- Wood frame and rug hook
- Staple gun and staples
- Black permanent felt pen
- Damp cloth and iron

Finished size: about 22 x 32½in/56 x 82.5cm

1 Stretch the burlap onto the wood frame with the straight grain parallel to the long sides. Start at one corner and staple along one long side, then work around the frame, stapling each side in turn.

2 Enlarge the template to the required size and transfer to the burlap, leaving a 2-4in/5-10cm border all around. To mark straight lines, draw the pen nib between two threads.

3 Select the wool fabric you need and cut it into ¼in/6mm strips. As a guide, you need to cut strips from a piece of fabric about four times the motif size to have enough strips to cover it.

4 Hold the hook as if you are holding a pen. Hold a strip of fabric between your finger and thumb on the under-side of the burlap. Push the hook firm-ly through the weave on the line at the corner of a motif and bring the end of the strip through to the right side.

5 Leaving the end on the top side, push the hook through the weave two threads away on the marked line and pull a small loop through to the top. The loop should be about ¼in/6mm high.

6 Continue around the edge of the motif, making loops of the same size every two threads. The wool strips should be close enough to cover the burlap, but not so close it bunches up.

7 Leave the end of each strip of wool on the top before starting a new strip as before. Work in lines echoing the out-side shape and work in towards the center to fill the shape completely.
(see picture next column)

8 Work the rest of the design in the same way. Once complete, carefully take the rug off the frame and press on the wrong side with a damp cloth and a hot iron.

9 Cut strips of twill tape to fit down each side. With right sides together, sew the twill tape to the burlap, close to the last row of hooking.

10 Trim the burlap to 1in/2.5cm and turn the tape over onto the wrong side. Miter the corners neatly and slip stitch in place.

11 Hem the twill tape to the wrong side of the rug.

candle sconce

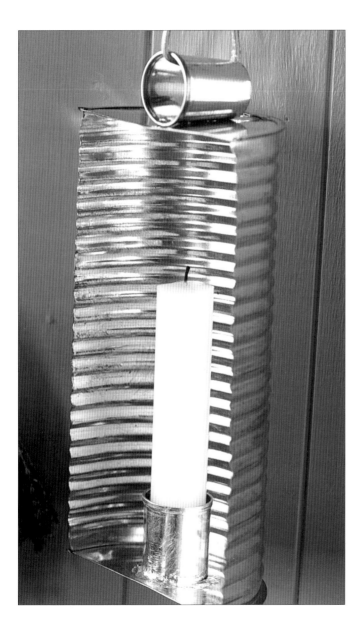

Candle sconces were very much a part of everyday Shaker life, though the Millenial Laws were strict about their use, recognizing the fire risk with so much wood used for furniture and buildings. Sconces were customarily made from tin in a variety of shapes, often curving round the candle holder to act as a reflector. The individual parts of the sconce were cut out of tin plate and then crimped if necessary, before being soldered together.

The Shakers were some of the most progressive people of their day and their workshops were like small factories with the most advanced power-driven machinery. In 1800, a huge water-powered trip hammer was set up in New Lebanon, New York, to pound metal into shape; later, it was adapted to pound ash logs for basketwork.

This candle sconce has been put together from ready-made pieces. The holder and handle are plain round pastry cutters and the reflector is a specialist baking tin used to make the distinctive shape of Stollen or milk bread. Use a resin core solder to make the task easier, and remember to heat the metal – rather than the solder – to achieve a firm join.

▶ 9 3

Hang the candle from a loop of leather cord, or stand it
on a table with its back to the draft.

A Stollen baking tin is perfect for this project, but if you can't find one, you could cut a tall tin can in half to achieve the same shape. Turn and hammer the sharp cut edges to the inside before fitting the candle holder and handle.

BASIC METALWORKING SKILLS
AND KNOWLEDGE OF POWER TOOLS
REQUIRED

MATERIALS
◆ *Semicircular Stollen or milk bread baking tin*
◆ *Two small round pastry cutters*
◆ *Soldering iron and resin core flux*
◆ *⅛in/3mm drill bit and drill*
◆ *⅛in/3mm short aluminum rivets and rivet gun*
◆ *Sanding block*
◆ *Clean rag*
◆ *Pencil*
◆ *Masking tape*
◆ *Length of leather cord*

Finished size: 4⅛ x 9⅜ in/10.5 x 24cm

1 Stand the baking tin on end and sand down the inside and the sharp edge of one pastry cutter to clean the surface thoroughly. Wipe with the rag.

2 Heat the soldering iron. Position the cutter inside the baking tin and secure with a tab of tape inside the cutter, near the front.

3 Use the soldering iron to heat the metal where the two pieces join and apply a dot of solder inside on the back edge of the cutter. Apply dots of solder round the front edge of the cutter until it is secured.

4 Use the tip of the soldering iron to smooth the solder neatly round the front edge. Drill two ⅛in/3mm holes on one side of the other pastry cutter.

5 Hold the cutter in position on top of the baking tin and mark the hole positions. Drill two matching holes in the tin.

6 Working from inside the tin, and keeping the two pieces in position, use a rivet gun to insert rivets in the holes.

7 Thread a length of leather cord through the cutter and tie a secure knot.

alphabet
board

Education was provided in the Shaker communities for both believers and non-believers by some of the Brothers and Sisters. Boys attended school in winter, girls in summer, and each term lasted four months. Every child had a miniature blackboard made from slate set in a narrow pine frame that was marked discreetly with their initials. Large hand painted alphabet boards were hung in the school rooms to help the children learn the proper formation of letters and numbers. These were about 3¼yd/3m long and reversible, with a simple style of writing for young children on one side and a cursive alphabet for older students on the other.

This project combines the letters and slate ideas to make a unique family memo or bulletin board. The letters and numbers are traced onto thin paper and painted black before being cut out. This method solves the problem of the brush slipping, as any mistakes can be trimmed off before the perfect shapes are stuck in position on the painted frame. Several coats of matte varnish ensure that they look quite authentically hand painted.

The alphabet board is designed to be hung on the wall, but better still, if you have the space, it would look perfect leaning against an easel.

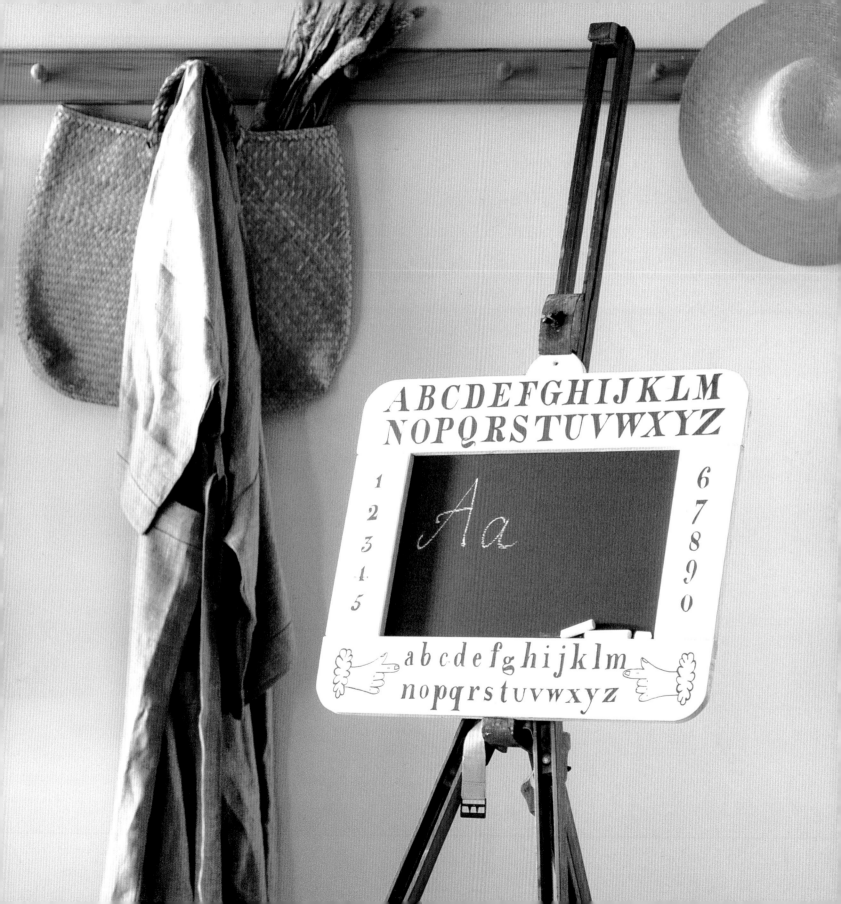

The alphabet board looks meticulously hand painted but instead it is made by cutting out pre-painted templates. The painted paper letters are glued on and covered with several coats of matte varnish to complete the illusion.

BASIC WOODWORKING SKILLS AND KNOWLEDGE OF POWER TOOLS REQUIRED

MATERIALS
◆ 39in/1m of ½ x 3½in/12 x 90mm pine
◆ 20in/500mm of ½ x 6in/12 x 150mm pine
◆ 17 x 13in/430 x 330mm of ¼in/6mm MDF
◆ Basic tool kit (see page 10)
◆ Band, fret or jigsaw
◆ Blackboard paint
◆ Off white matte acrylic paint
◆ Matte acrylic varnish
◆ Paintbrushes
◆ Scissors and PVA glue
◆ Black permanent felt pen
◆ Set of compasses and pencil
◆ Coffee mug, 2¾in/70mm in diameter
◆ Length of cord

Finished size (excluding hanging support): 15¾ x 19¾in/400 x 500mm

1 Mark a line 3½in/90mm from the bottom edge of the wider pine. With the point of the compasses in the center point of the line, draw a semicircle with a 1½in/40mm radius above the line. At each end of the plank, use the mug to draw a quarter circle below the line.

2 From the ½ x 3½in/12 x 90mm pine, saw two side pieces 8¼in/210mm long and a 20in/500mm piece for the bottom of the frame. Use the mug to draw quarter circles on the bottom corners as before.

3 Saw along the marked lines to shape the top and bottom sections. Sand the edges of the wood to round them off slightly. Drill and countersink a ¼in/6mm hole in the center of the semi-circle.

4 Paint the 4 sections off-white and leave to dry. Paint the MDF on one side with two coats of blackboard paint.

5 Enlarge the templates at the back of the book until the capitals are 1⅛in/30mm high, and the lower case letters and numbers ¾-1⅛in/20-30mm high. Transfer onto paper. Paint the letters and numbers with blackboard paint or color with felt pen. Cut each one out carefully and arrange them on the frame sections. Glue in position.

6 Trace the hand shape and draw around it on either side of the lower case letters. Paint or color with felt pen. When dry, apply two coats of varnish to each section.

7 Assemble the frame face down on a flat surface, with the numbers 1-5 on the right and 6-0 on the left. Tape the frame together. Place the MDF on top, paint side down. Mark the corners and where to drill the screw holes, two on each side.

8 Lift the MDF off, then drill and countersink the screw holes. Reposition the MDF and drill shallow pilot holes into the pine. Remove the tape carefully and screw the blackboard in position. Tie a cord through the hole to hang.

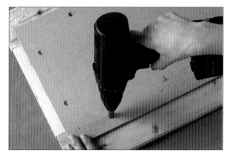

knitted throw

In general, Shakers learned several skills because Mother Ann Lee believed that "variety of occupation is a source of pleasure." This diversity of skills was practical, allowing one member of the community to step in for another during times of ill health, and it also meant that some tasks – such as knitting – could be fitted around other work. The Sisters spun and dyed their own wool, winding it into balls using a table swift. They produced a range of knitted goods such as mittens, socks, stockings, sweaters, and rugs. Their thick, water-resistant mittens were made larger than required and then shrunk to fit over a wooden mitt shape.

This knitted throw is knitted from 100% pure new wool and is the size of a square blanket. I chose wool in a quiet tweed color which suits the utilitarian nature of the article. The overall pattern is a simple check made from two basic knitting stitches – moss stitch and stocking stitch – knitted on a circular needle. Stocking stitch is worked by alternating a row of purl and a row of plain stitches, whereas moss stitch alternates knit and purl stitches in the same row.

The basic pattern of the throw is a four-square stocking stitch block, edged by a chunky border of moss stitch.

This throw is knitted in one piece on circular knitting needles. These needles can accommodate a large number of stitches but you knit in the same way as with straight needles. Check your knitting often and correct any mistakes before continuing.

BASIC KNITTING SKILLS REQUIRED

MATERIALS
◆ *Circular knitting needles US 8(¼ x 31½in)/UK 6(5 x 800mm)*
◆ *Eight 4oz/100g skeins of 100% pure new wool Rowan Magpie Tweed*
◆ *Scissors*
◆ *Large tapestry needle*

Finished size: about 43in/110cm square

1 Cast on 175 stitches.

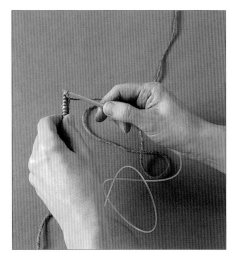

2 Work 16 rows of moss stitch. To do this, knit one, purl one across the row, beginning with a knit stitch on every row.

3 Work 10 stitches in moss stitch to make the border. Pattern row 1: knit 17 stitches, purl 1, knit 17, work 5 stitches in moss stitch. Repeat the pattern three times and then finish the row in moss stitch.

4 Work 10 stitches in moss stitch. Pattern row 2: purl 35 stitches, moss stitch 5. Repeat the pattern three times and then finish the row in moss stitch.

5 Continue alternating the two pattern rows until 25 rows have been completed, ending on the second pattern row. Work a row of moss stitch.

6 Work the two pattern rows alternately for a further 25 rows, ending on the second pattern row. Work 6 rows of moss stitch.

7 This forms the check pattern for the entire throw. Continue until there are four rows of four large check squares. Tie in new skeins of wool on the wrong side. *(see picture next column)*

8 End on a second pattern row and then work 16 rows of moss stitch.

9 Cast off loosely. Untie the knots and sew the ends of the wool into the throw on the wrong side. Press the throw lightly on the wrong side using a damp cloth.

templates

quilt

enlarge to about 10in/25cm square

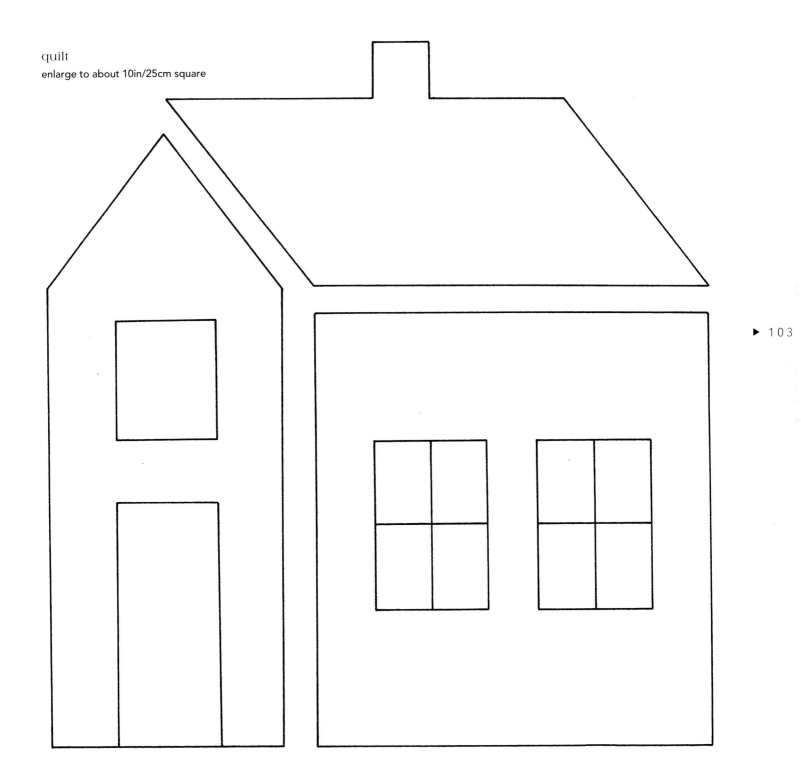

table runner

enlarge to about 16in/40cm at its widest point

pillow case

diagram for hem stitch

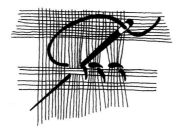

S H A K E R

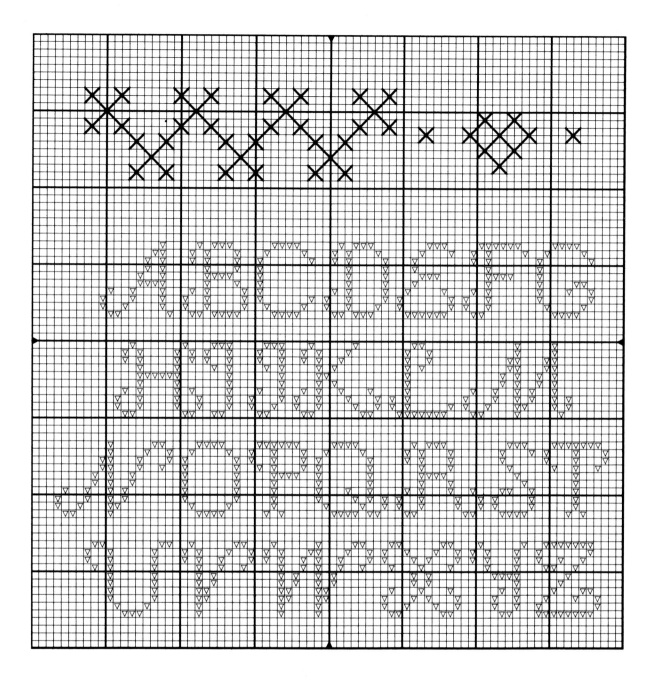

166

167

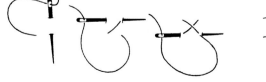

168

hand towel and toilet bag
diagrams for marking cross stitch
showing front and reverse sides

TEMPLATES

pie safe
enlarge to height of 9½in/24cm

towel rail
enlarge longest length to 6¼in/258mm

S H A K E R

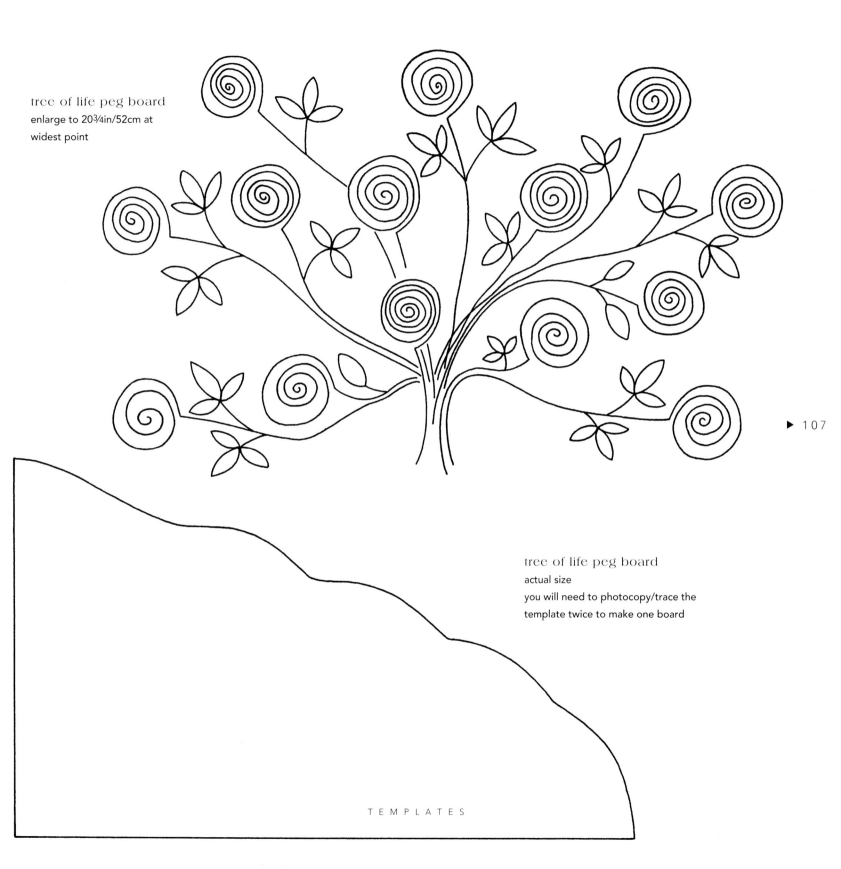

tree of life peg board
enlarge to 20¾in/52cm at
widest point

tree of life peg board
actual size
you will need to photocopy/trace the
template twice to make one board

TEMPLATES

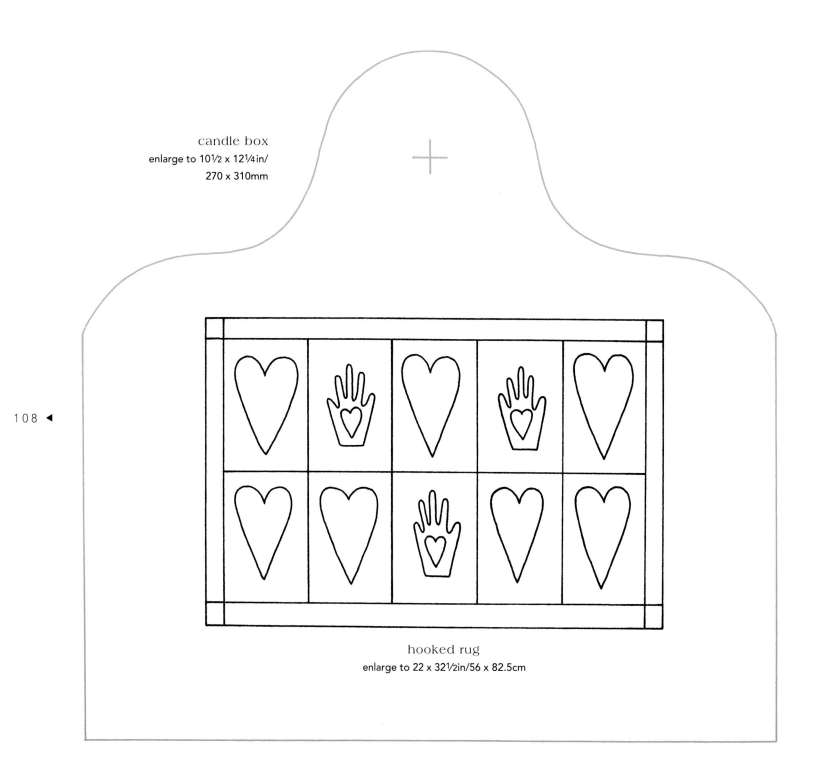

candle box
enlarge to 10½ x 12¼in/
270 x 310mm

hooked rug
enlarge to 22 x 32½in/56 x 82.5cm

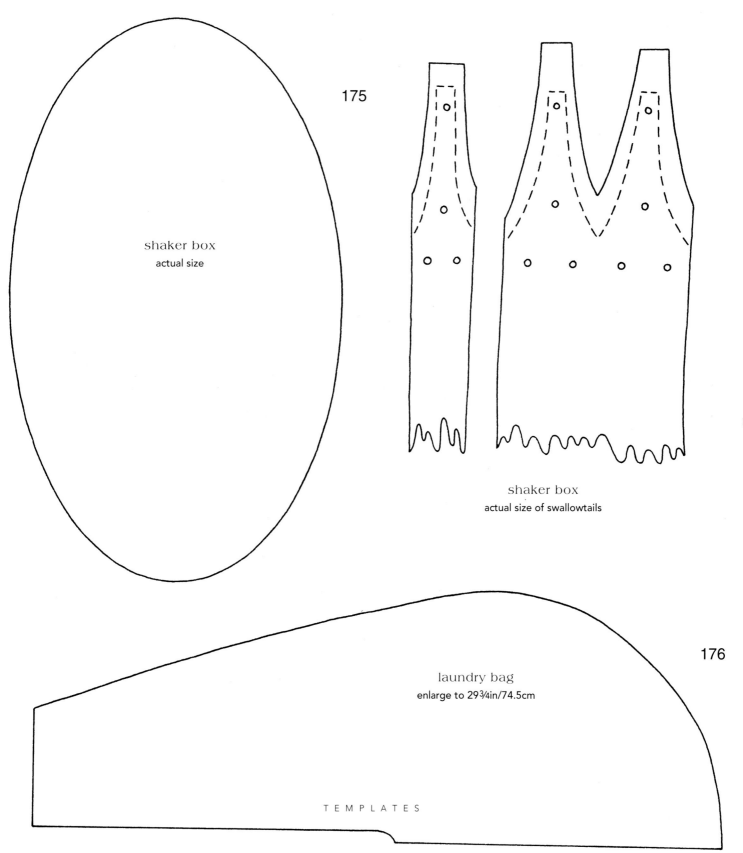

shaker box
actual size

shaker box
actual size of swallowtails

laundry bag
enlarge to 29¾in/74.5cm

175

176

▶ 109

TEMPLATES

abcdefghijklmno
pqrstuvwxyz
1234567890

alphabet board
enlarge letters and numbers to about 1¼in/3cm tall

hand actual size

ABCDEFGHI
JKLMNOPQR
STUVWXYZ

source list

• ACE HARDWARE
Rocklin, CA, (916) 632-2200
call for store locations
General hardware, birch ply

• BRITEX FABRICS
San Francisco, CA, (415) 392-2910
A wide selection of fabrics, sewing
supplies, and notions

• CANE AND BASKET
Los Angeles, CA, (323) 939-9644
Lapping and flat bed cane

• CURRY'S ART SUPPLIES
Mississauga, Ontario (905) 272-4460
call for store locations
Craft and design supplies

• FLAX ART & DESIGN
San Francisco, CA, (800) 547-7778
Art and craft supplies

• INNOVATION SPECIALTIES
Culver City, CA, (800) 421-4445
Clock components

• JANOVIC/PLAZA INC.
Long Island City, NY, (800) 772-4381
Specialty decorating supplies

• JO-ANN FABRICS AND CRAFTS
Hudson, OH, (330) 656-2600
Muslin, warm and natural batting,
check and stripe fabrics

• MAXWELL FABRICS
Vancouver, BC, (800) 663-1159

• METAL SUPERMARKETS HAYWARD LTD.
Hayward, CA, (800) 700-2839
www.metalsupermarkets.com
Tin plate, pewter foil, galvanized wire

• MICHAEL'S
(800) MICHAELS, www.michaels.com
call for store locations
Craft and hobby supplies, hooks and
frames for hooked rug making

• PEARL PAINT
New York, NY, (800) 451-7327
Art supplies

• SHAKER WORKSHOPS
Arlington, MA, (800) 840-9121
Call for catalog of Shaker furniture
and accessories

• UTRECHT
Central, NJ, (800) 223-9132
Art supplies

index